MW00721442

A Fresh Anointing

OTHER AVAILABLE BOOKS
BY DR. AND MRS. JACK SCHAAP

Dating with a Purpose
(Common Sense Dating Principles for Couples,
Parents, and Youth Workers)
by Dr. Jack Schaap

Making Wise the Simple
by Dr. Jack Schaap

Marriage: God's Original Intent
by Dr. Jack Schaap

Preparing for Marriage
by Dr. Jack Schaap

A Wife's Purpose
by Cindy Schaap

A Meek and Quiet Spirit
(Lessons for Wives and Mothers
from Women in the New Testament)
by Cindy Schaap

Silk and Purple
(Lessons for Wives and Mothers
from Women in the Old Testament)
by Cindy Schaap

A Fresh Anointing

by
Dr. Jack Schaap

Pastor, First Baptist Church
of Hammond, Indiana

HYLES PUBLICATIONS • HAMMOND, INDIANA

COPYRIGHT © 2003
HYLES PUBLICATIONS

1st Printing–March 2003
2nd Printing–February 2004

Scriptures are taken from the King James Bible.

CREDITS:
PROJECT MANAGER: Dr. Bob Marshall
ASSISTANTS: Rochelle Chalifoux, Kristi Wertz
PAGE DESIGN AND LAYOUT: Linda Stubblefield
PROOFREADING: Debbie Borsh, Rena Fish,
Linda Flesher, Martha Gilbert, Jack Mitchell,
Julie Richter, and Vicki Siebenhaar
COVER DESIGN: Linda Stubblefield

To order additional books by Dr. Jack Schaap,
please contact:
HYLES PUBLICATIONS
523 Sibley Street
Hammond, Indiana 46320
Website: www.hylespublications.com
E-mail: info@hylespublications.com

Dedication

■ ■ ■

When I was a college preacher boy, a powerful and dynamic preacher from Hyles-Anderson College became the new pastor at my home church in Holland, Michigan. During a Christmas holiday, he invited me to his office. When I sat down, he looked at me and said, "Jack, are you filled with the Holy Spirit?" Wow! I had never been asked that before. My mind was spinning, looking for the proper answer. I shot back, "I don't know; are you?" He responded, "I'll ask the questions here in my office." I fell in love with him immediately. Here was a man who was talking right at my heart's door. Here was a man who preached powerfully and with great conviction. Here was a man who could steer me in the right direction.

His next question was equally unsettling. "Why aren't you attending Hyles-Anderson College?"

I responded, "My former pastor told me to attend where I am now."

He instantly commanded, "I'm your pastor now. Why aren't you attending Hyles-Anderson College?" I felt God had just stepped into my life and was very deliberately taking over the steering wheel of my life, and I was ready for the ride!

So began the journey that brought me eventually to the pulpit of the First Baptist Church of Hammond. I did attend Hyles-Anderson College. I also began a personal pursuit for the fullness of the Holy Spirit. I think it is no coincidence that I found that for which I was hungering, the power of the Holy Spirit, at the college my pastor advised me to attend. God used my pastor and his provocative questions and his wise counsel to bring me ultimately to that wonderful place called the perfect will of God for my life.

How I thank God for Spirit-filled preaching! How I thank God for a Spirit-filled pastor! How I thank God for a college that taught me to be a Spirit-filled preacher! How I thank God for His Spirit fullness on my ministry!

With my deepest gratitude, I dedicate this book to
DR. JAMES D. BINNEY

Thank you for provoking me to pursue a life of being filled with the Holy Spirit, and thank you for directing me to Hyles-Anderson College. Those two decisions have made all the difference in my Christian life. I love you, Brother Binney.

Table of Contents

Table of Contents *(continued)*

■   ■   ■

CHAPTER ONE

A Fresh Anointing

■　　■　　■

Acts 4:23-31, "*And being let go, they went to their own company, and reported all that the chief priests and elders had
said unto them. And when they heard that, they lifted up
their voice to God with one accord, and said, Lord, thou art God,
which hast made heaven, and earth, and the sea, and all that in
them is: Who by the mouth of thy servant David hast said, Why
did the heathen rage, and the people imagine vain things? The kings
of the earth stood up, and the rulers were gathered together against
the Lord, and against his Christ. For of a truth against thy holy
child Jesus, whom thou hast anointed, both Herod, and Pontius
Pilate, with the Gentiles, and the people of Israel, were gathered
together, For to do whatsoever thy hand and thy counsel determined
before to be done. And now, Lord, behold their threatenings: and
grant unto thy servants, that with all boldness they may speak thy
word, By stretching forth thine hand to heal; and that signs and
wonders may be done by the name of thy holy child Jesus. And when
they had prayed, the place was shaken where they were assembled
together; and they were all filled with the Holy Ghost, and they
spake the word of God with boldness.*"

In those early days, the local church was struggling to

get established. In Acts 1, a little New Testament group of believers numbered 120 in the city of Jerusalem—that hardened, dangerous city where the officials had just allowed the murder of the Lord Jesus Christ a few weeks before. In the first seven chapters of the book of Acts, within a space of two years, that church grew to many tens of thousands of members. That fact can be proven Biblically. Dr. Curtis Hutson said that he would estimate the number of believers very conservatively at just under 100,000 members in that church at Jerusalem. What explosive growth in a hard, difficult city—if there's any such thing as an "easy" city.

When I was 17 years old, I was preparing to go either to the Air Force Academy or in business with my father. Dad had offered me a tremendous opportunity to be in business with him.

During September of my senior year of high school, my pastor asked my family if we would host Dr. Carl Boonstra, a preacher from the Baptist Bible Fellowship in Springfield, Missouri. While we were at a restaurant, Dr. Boonstra sat on my right. During the meal, he looked at me and asked, "Jack, how old are you?"

I said, "I'm 16 years old."

"Are you a sophomore or a junior?"

"No," I said, "I'm a senior in high school."

"What are you going to do when you graduate?"

I replied, "I'm going to go into business with my dad, I think."

He said that plan sounded like a good idea. Then he added, "Have you ever thought about full-time Christian service?"

When Dr. Boonstra asked that question, I felt a tug on my heart. I couldn't quite figure out what it was, but it was like an itch I couldn't scratch because it was in my spirit— in my heart! It was not something I understood at that time, but the tug was there. I said, "No, Sir. I have never thought about full-time Christian service."

He said, "Would you do me a favor?"

I said, "Sure, Dr. Boonstra! Anything you want."

"Would you pray about it?"

I'll be honest; I didn't want to pray too much about serving God full-time. After all, I had heard that when a person prays, things tend to happen. I didn't want things to happen! But I had promised him I'd pray about it, so on the way to the car, I said, "God, Dr. Boonstra asked me to pray about full-time Christian service, so I am. Amen." Literally, that was my prayer. I didn't want to pray too much, but I had promised to pray about it, so now I did.

Through September, October, November, December, and January, I forgot about my promise to pray. In February, Evangelist Gary Gilmore was traveling through my hometown with his travel trailer. Because Dad owned and operated a mobile home park, and since there was an open lot, Brother Gilmore parked his travel trailer on that lot. February in Michigan brings snow and freezing temperatures. About 1 o'clock or 2 o'clock in the morning, a knock sounded on our door, and a voice was calling, "Mr. Schaap, Mr. Schaap!"

Dad went to the door and found Brother Gilmore standing there. Dad woke me and said, "Get dressed, Son. We've got to help Brother Gilmore. The pipes in his travel trailer have frozen. We need to thaw out their facilities."

Dad told Brother Gilmore to unhook his travel trailer and pull it into one of our garage bays. Dad turned on the heat, and he and I crawled on our backs under the trailer holding power hoses that forced hot air on the undercarriage of the trailer. Brother Gilmore said to me, "I sure appreciate your helping me out."

I said, "We're glad to do it, Brother Gilmore."

He said, "By the way, what are you doing this year? Are you in school?"

I said, "Yes, Sir."

He asked, "What year are you in school?"

I answered, "I am a senior."

He said, "What will you be doing when you graduate?"

I said, "I'm going to go into business with my dad."

He said, "That sounds like a good idea. Have you ever prayed about full-time Christian service?"

"Yes, I have! I already prayed about that and I took care of it," I assured him.

He asked, "What happened?"

"Oh, nothing," I said, "I'm going to go into business with my dad."

He asked, "Would you do me a favor?"

I said, "Sure, Brother Gilmore, anything you want."

He said, "Would you pray about it again?"

Once again, I felt that same tug at my heart. Something began itching. It was just like a little festering wound, but I couldn't figure out what it was, so I said, "Sure, I'll pray about it." Truthfully, when we finally solved the frozen pipe problem and when Dad and I were walking back into the house, I said, "Oh, Lord, I nearly forgot. I promised Brother Gilmore I'd pray about full-time Christian service, so I am, amen." Once again, I didn't want to pray about it too much; God seems to mess things up when you pray too much. That incident happened in February, and I soon forgot about it.

March passed, and in April, Dr. Jack Van Impe was scheduled to preach in the big civic auditorium in my hometown of Holland, Michigan. At that time, Dr. Van Impe was a fundamental Baptist evangelist who traveled the nation, holding big city-wide crusades. Since my home church was going to be the host church, my family helped with his personal transportation. I got to ride in the car with him, go out to eat with him, and have him sign my Bible. I got to know him. It was big league stuff for a teenager, and I had a delightful time.

His advance man arrived in town two weeks before Dr. Van Impe came, and he told our church how to prepare for this big city-wide crusade. The man said, "On a particular night, we're going to have a big youth night. We want to get all of the teenagers to come so we can get them all saved. Really publicize that night in the public high schools and get the teens excited about it."

So, I said to myself, "I've got two friends with whom I have gone through kindergarten, grade school, junior high, and high school. In fact, we are graduating together in two months. I've known them all of my life, but I don't know if they're saved. I think they are, but I want to be sure to get them saved." One friend's name was Jeff; and the other's name was Jerry. The three of us—Jerry, Jeff, and Jack—played on a hockey team together, rode motorcycles together, and played on a baseball team together. We just did everything together. I invited them to come to the city-wide crusade, and they said they would.

I picked up my friend Jerry and took him to the service that night. We sat way up in the balcony with Jeff. When the invitation came after a powerful sermon, neither one of my friends moved. I offered, "If you want to go...."

"No, I don't want to go...."

I said, "All right!"

At the close of the meeting, I told Jeff I'd see him at school the next day. As I drove Jerry to his home that night, my heart was burdened. My heart was just breaking for my best friends. Since the advance man for Brother Van Impe had come, I had been praying every night for two weeks for them. Sometimes I prayed 15 minutes, sometimes 30 minutes, and sometimes longer than an hour for my friends, Jerry and Jeff, to get saved.

The moment had arrived. I was in the driver's seat of my dad's pick-up truck, and Jerry was sitting in the passenger seat. "Before you leave, Jerry," I said, "tonight you heard a great preacher preach. Did you understand what he was saying?"

He said, "Yes, I did!"

I said, "You understand that if you don't get saved, you're going to go to Hell?"

He said, "Yes, I know that." Big tears began to well up in his eyes. Tears began to escape his eyes and run down his face. He reached for the door handle, and he said, "I've got to go." (It was the first time in my entire life that I had ever seen Jerry have tears.)

"Oh, don't go, Jerry," I begged. "Just another few minutes, please. Jerry, you've got to get saved."

He said, "I know! I know!"

"Get saved!"

He said, "No! No! No! Not tonight!"

I said, "Please get saved tonight, Jerry."

He said, "No! No! I can't!" He bolted out the truck door. I called behind him, "Jerry! Jerry! Before you go to bed, get on your knees, and ask the Lord to save you!"

He ran down the driveway and entered his house. I waited until I saw a light come on in his bedroom. I backed the truck out of the driveway with a heavy heart. I drove home, called my pastor, Charles Surrett, and said, "Brother Surrett, would you please pray for my friend? I'm worried that he is not going to get saved."

"I'll pray for him," he said. "I promise you, I'll spend a half an hour praying for him right now."

Oh, how I thank God for a good pastor who shared my burden and prayed that night. I spent about an hour or an hour and a half praying for Jerry that night.

I rose the next morning and went to high school. I was feeling a little embarrassed, and I wondered how my friends would respond to the message they had heard. That afternoon we worked together in a construction crew on a cooperative program where we received credit for building a house.

As usual, we ate lunch in Jerry's car. Jerry was in the driver's seat and always had the radio on—listening to music. I'd sit in the passenger seat, and Jeff would sit behind me.

Suddenly, Jerry reached over, shut off the music, and put down his sandwich. He said, "Jack, I've got to tell you something."

Honestly, I was scared. I thought he might tell me he didn't appreciate my putting pressure on him.

Instead, he said, "Last night, after you dropped me off at the house, I got on my knees, and I asked Jesus to come into my heart and save me."

I declared, "Jerry, that's just the best news I ever heard in my life! I'm so proud of you!"

He said, "Well, thanks for taking me. I appreciate it."

Jeff leaned forward, and he said, "Hey! You did that?"

He said, "Yeah! Why?"

He said, "I did the same thing last night. I went home, got on my knees before I went to bed, and I got saved, too."

I was happy! I was excited! I thought, "That's just a good feeling all over." There is no feeling like getting your friends saved!

I went home that night and, for probably half an hour before I went to bed, thanked God for saving my friends. The next night I got out of bed and said, "God, I just want to thank You again for getting my friends saved." I spent probably an hour just thanking Him and praising Him and fellowshipping with the Lord.

The next night I was up for about an hour and a half praying. The following night I spent two hours with God. All the rest of that week, I stayed up an hour or an hour and a half. The next week, I continued the practice of being up for an hour to an hour and a half.

About May 6, I remember that I was praying at about 1:30 in the morning. I can still picture the incident in my mind. The whole room lit up with the presence of God. I cannot explain nor totally describe what happened.

I have since heard and read stories of other people who had experienced the same presence of God. I just can't explain what happened, but it was as if God moved into that room. I felt like I was literally going to die. I was so overwhelmed with the awareness of God's presence. I read later about a person who described the occurrence like this: "I felt like I was drowning in liquid waves of love."

When I read that sentence, I said, "That's exactly what I felt like." I felt like I was in a sea of God's love, and I was drowning in it. It was the most wonderful way to go, and I thought, "I'm literally going to die!"

I was reminded of the story about D. L. Moody when he was on Wall Street. He was asking for money for his schools when suddenly a mighty enduement of power from the Spirit of God fell upon him. Mr. Moody said that he had to find a place to run to in the middle of the city. Tears were streaming down his face. He had to find some place to get alone with God just to say, "God, wait a minute. I'm dying while feeling Your presence, and I don't want to lose it."

That's how it was that night for me. It was a wonderful, special, unique, indescribable, one-of-a-kind experience.

I don't know how long I was awake that night. I might have been up past three, four, or five o'clock. I don't know. I don't remember going to bed that night. All I can remember is that when it was time to get up, I got dressed, opened my door, and made my way into the hallway. My mom was standing there, and she shared with me the miracle story about how she had prayed on a hospital bed after a devastating car accident that nearly took her life and had left her critically injured to have a son who would be a preacher.

In that room that night, God stepped in and did something. This business of serving God is a very real thing to me because it is about souls! It is about Heaven! It is about the baptism of the power of God!

Of course, I'm not talking about simply an emotional experience or some religious wildfire; I'm talking about a real God Who wrote a real Book, Who is alive, and Who wants to do something special in every Christian's life.

I was called to preach that night. I don't believe God spoke audibly to me, though He could have if He had chosen to do so. I believe I already have God's Words in my King James Bible. God spoke to me, "Jack, I want you to preach for Me," and I said, "I'd do anything for You, God." I yielded. The soul and spirit of a man knitted with the Spirit of God—just like a bond. The most intimate bond in the universe is the bond between man and God!

Something happened to me that night. I told my dad, and he said, "You've got to go to college."

I had argued with Dad before when he told me I had to go, but now when he said I had to go, I said, "I know. I've got to go to that college in Minnesota. But Dad, I've never been there. I don't know anything about it. What's it like?"

He said, "I don't know, but your pastor told you to go. Why don't you go and try it?"

I said, "Yes, sir. I will."

God took a young man and put him alone at that school. I got to that school, and I was the only person in the world I knew there. I was scared and lonely. Every night for the first month, I wept myself to sleep. I roomed with two other young men. In a room with bunk beds stacked three high, mine was the bottom bunk. At night, I'd bury my head in my pillow so the guys above me would not hear me. (They were probably crying and were scared I'd hear them!) I would put my head in my pillow, and I'd just weep. I was so lonely and so homesick; and frankly, I just did not want to be there.

I have some wonderful memories and wonderful friends of a lifetime from the time I attended that college for God sent me there. The school was not what we are here at First Baptist Church; it used to be years ago, but it wasn't when I attended there. That's not a critical statement. It's just a statement of fact. It was different, but God sent me there.

One day when my roommates were out of the room and the tears were running down my face, I picked up my Bible. I knelt and said, "Lord, I'm so lonely and homesick here. God, it's not that I don't want to be here. I'm not unhappy that I'm here. I just don't know anybody. The only person I know is You, and the only Book I have is this one. God, if You don't do something for me, I don't think I'm going to make it. God, I can handle the academic load. I can put a smile on my face in the hallway. I can shake people's hands, but God, I am not a social person. This ministry business isn't for me. I don't like crowds. I don't like being with people. I just want to go back home, walk in the woods, and meet with You." I opened my Bible and said, "God, if You don't speak to me through this Book and make it real to me, I don't know if I can make it."

I went to the library and began reading biographies like the story of Charles G. Finney. I read about this great lawyer, Charles Finney, who got saved. He had a powerful conversion testimony. He wrote that after his conversion the Spirit of God came over him again and again. He was just overwhelmed with the awareness of God's presence in his life. He was overwhelmed that God loved him, and he was overwhelmed that sinners needed Christ. He had never had a happening like that before, but he began to experience God's working through him. He met a man in the street and simply called his name. The man stopped, looked at him, and began to weep. He got on his knees and said, "Charles, I need what you have."

I read those stories that burned in my heart nearly 27 years ago. I have been reading those stories again. I re-read the story of how Charles Finney was on a tour with a friend. He walked into a textile mill where cloth was manufactured. The noisy machines would have made it impossible to speak to the workers. He quietly walked into a large room where many women were working at noisy looms. When they spotted Finney, they giggled and laughed at him. They began to gather together and talk about him. Finney said, "I felt very uncomfortable. I felt like they were making fun of me and snickering at me. I stopped walking. I didn't speak one word. I just stopped and looked at them. As I looked at them, one woman went back to work. She became nervous and broke the thread on her loom. As she tried to put it together, the tears began to run down her cheeks, and she fell on her face. The other women came to her side, dropped to their knees, and before I knew it, they were all lying on their faces crying. I hadn't yet said one word. I hadn't said, 'Hello!' or 'Good morning,' because I couldn't have been heard if I had tried to speak."

Suddenly the owner came in with the superintendent. The superintendent happened to be a saved man. The owner was a lost man, and as he looked around, the owner said, "What's wrong here! Why aren't these people working?"

The superintendent said, "Looks like they're praying." He looked at me and said, "Mr. Finney, what's going on?"

I said, "I walked into the room, and that's what happened."

"What did you say?"

I said, "I didn't say a thing!"

The superintendent said, "Shut down the factory and turn off the machines. Let's get everyone together in the big room and let's preach to them."

That meeting went on for that entire day, all night, and all the next day! The owner got saved, and all of the workers got saved.

When I read that, I said, "That's what I want!" I don't need to walk into a room and have that happen, but I want to be used of God. I want to have the mighty power of God. I want that baptism of the Spirit of God!

Hey, all of you charismatics! Stop your jabbering in tongues! Why don't you get baptized in the Spirit of God and get people saved?

Another story I read about Charles Finney recounted how he was preaching in a city, when a great revival broke out. An old man came in and asked Mr. Finney to preach in his community, where a religious service with preaching had never been held.

Mr. Finney asked how to get to his community. When the elderly gentleman gave him directions, Mr. Finney wrote them down on a piece of paper and promised to be there the next evening to preach. Since Mr. Finney had no transportation, he walked. It was a hot day and by the time he arrived, he was exhausted from the heat. Mr. Finney said he was so discouraged in his spirit that he wondered why he had gone there in the first place. He didn't know those people.

When Mr. Finney finally arrived, he walked inside a building and heard the people cussing and swearing. Everywhere he walked in the town, he heard profanity. He was so bothered by their vile language that his heart was burdened for the people and their need to know God.

The next day, Mr. Finney met with a man from the town, and they planned a meeting. A handful of people came to hear the preaching. Not much happened at the service. The next service was held the next morning, and quite a large crowd turned out. Charles Finney decided to preach on the story of Sodom and Gomorrah. What he didn't know was that the name of the city where he was preaching was Sodom!

Mr. Finney related how the profanity of the people in Sodom angered God. The townspeople began to glare at Mr. Finney. He couldn't understand why the people were so upset over a Bible story!

He told them how the only righteous man in the town of Sodom was a man named Lot. Mr. Finney could not have known that the old man who came and got him from the city where he was preaching was named Lot! He had not asked the man for his name!

Mr. Finney told how God was going to rain fire and brimstone on Sodom. Halfway through his sermon, a bunch of those mean guys fell on their faces. The only person sitting on his chair was the old man named Lot. One after another got saved until all of the people were saved.

After the revival, Mr. Finney asked, "Why did the people get so angry at me?"

An older citizen responded, "Because our city is named Sodom, and the only man who was saved in this town was Lot. They thought you came gunning for them."

Mr. Finney said, "I didn't know that!"

Once again the power of God fell! Many years later, the power of God was still evident in the town of Sodom.

I also read the stories of Mr. Finney holding meetings sometimes eight or nine weeks long. He conducted a meeting in New York City where just under 100,000 people got saved. Sometime at those meetings, nobody had arrived when it was time for the meeting to start. He thought the people were angry at him but people began to drift in late. They called, "Mr. Finney! Would you come out here! The people can't get through because so many carriages are stopped in the road."

People had left their carriages and had fallen on their faces in the middle of the road to pray because they were already under such conviction. Many times a meeting was conducted in the streets or highways because the people couldn't get to the meeting house because they were so convicted. Can you imagine stopping on Sibley Street and getting on your face? Sounds kind of dangerous!

I kept reading biographies, and I was captivated by D. L. Moody. I learned how every time he preached, two women in his church would meet him in the back of the auditorium to say, "Fine sermon, Mr. Moody. We're praying for you, sir."

Finally, he stopped them to ask, "Why are you praying for me?"

They said, "We're praying that you'll know the baptism of the Holy Spirit."

He said, "We always have people saved; we always have a good service."

He realized that something was missing in his preaching, so he began begging God for His power. One day, he found it on Wall Street. God opened the windows of Heaven and poured out mighty spiritual influence on Mr. Moody. Whereas before that time five or six people were saved, now he had 40, 50, or 60 people getting saved in the services.

As I read those biographies, I said to my roommate, "Bob, would you enter into a covenant with me? I want to get up at 4 o'clock every morning, and I want to be downstairs in those empty classrooms by 4:30, and I want to pray until 7:30. Would you enter into an agreement that you will do that with me? I want you to pray with me. If we'll get up together, we'll motivate each other. When I'm tired, you get me up. When you're tired, I'll get you up."

Bob agreed, and we began to pray. At 4 o'clock we got up and at 4:30 we were in the classroom. Three hours! The sweet memories remain of day after day after day after day from 4:30 to 5:00 to 5:30 to 6:00 to 6:30 to 7:00 to 7:30, and sometimes at about 7:45 a.m., we would still be praying when the students started filtering in for 8:00 classes.

"Jack, you've got to get out of here. It's time for class," Bob would say.

"Just a few more minutes," I'd beg.

A senior named Dave checked our dormitory room every night. He would open the door, count the fellows to see if we were all in our room. I got to know Dave quite well. As he checked our room every night, he would ask, "Hey, Jack! Any wisdom you've got today?"

I always replied in the negative, but after several weeks, Bob said, "Tell him, Jack! Tell him what you've been doing."

"Tell him what?"

"Tell him about your early morning prayer meetings," Bob urged.

"Nah, I'm not going to tell him about that."

Dave asked, "What prayer meeting? What are you doing?"

When I said, "Oh, nothing," Bob said, "Oh, tell him you get up at 4 o'clock every morning and pray from 4:30 to 7:30."

Dave immediately said, "You can't do that! Nobody in college does that! We don't have time to do that!"

I declared, "I do! I'm a preacher! I'm going to make time for God! I don't care if it takes me forever to get through college. I want the power of God in my life. I've been reading these books about Finney and Moody. I've learned about the power of God through the printed page! When I got called to preach, God met me; and when I preach, I want God to use me! I want the power of God on my life."

He asked, "How do you pray three hours?"

I said, "Try it."

Dave said, "I can't!"

I dared Dave a couple of times, and he accepted the challenge. He came back two weeks later and said, "You have revolutionized my life!"

I was quick to maintain, "No, I didn't; God did!"

He asked, "Would you share what you just told me two weeks ago to all the guys on this floor?"

"I'll be glad to," I agreed.

He set up a floor meeting for me, and I met with about 30 men to share with them what Bob and I had done. They all became excited about it. As they began to pray, God began to meet with them. The news soon spread across that campus about so many young men praying on the campus!

About two weeks after that, Dave asked, "Jack, would you ever be interested in speaking to the entire dorm? I believe I could arrange to have all of the guys in the dorm for a one-time meeting together. Would you speak to an entire dorm like you did to me?"

When I agreed, he said, "They're waiting for you right now!"

I was ready for bed, sitting in my bathrobe. I wanted to wait until the next week, but Dave urged me to come right then.

I was overwhelmed with the thought of speaking to a couple hundred guys. I walked into a huge room with guys lined up around the walls, some sitting on chairs and sofas and some sitting on the floor. Many were yawning, and I heard some comments like, "Let's get this over with! Who are you? You're a brand new guy! What are you doing here? What do you want to say?"

As I waited, I prayed and said, "God, I'm just going to tell them what You've been doing."

Dave quieted the group and said, "Let me have your attention, please. About three or four weeks ago, this young man challenged me about praying and getting the fullness of the Spirit. Would you please give him a hearing? He'll just take five or ten minutes. Jack...."

I stood, but I didn't really know what to say. As I looked around the room, I knew many of the men by name. I said, "Fellows, we're all preachers, aren't we? Isn't that why we came? We need the power of God on our lives. If we don't have the power of God on our lives, we are failures because the only Person who can help us is God Almighty.

I began calling several of their names, pleading and admonishing them to seek the fullness of the Holy Spirit. We met for about 20 minutes. I had never been in a service like that one in my life. One of the men began to sob uncontrollably. He ran out of the room all the way down four levels to the basement. Four levels above I could hear his cries, "OH, GOD! OH, GOD! I WANT THE POWER OF GOD! OH, GOD! I DON'T WANT TO BE POWERLESS! OH, GOD! THAT YOUNG MAN IS RIGHT!"

It felt like a knife went through that room. Those young men fell prostrate on the floor and wept. They ran to their rooms. They left and found empty places. They sought any quiet place they could to be alone. The sounds of 200 college boys weeping and wailing and begging for the power of God began to permeate that whole dormitory. You could hear them for hour after hour. I stayed with Dave in that meeting room for hours with tears streaming down my face. Dave kept saying, "This is what we wanted! We want the power of God in this place. We want the soul-winning power! We want the baptism of the Holy Spirit!"

I agreed, "That's right, Dave."

The next day I was supposed to preach out of town at a Christian school. While I was gone, the college called an emergency session of chapel. I returned from preaching in the middle of the service, and the school seemed deserted. I noticed a custodian and asked, "What's going on?"

"Oh, the administration has called an emergency chapel."

When I asked, "Why?" the custodian said, "Where have you been? Last night some young guy got carried away preaching, and the dorm was awake all night with weeping and wailing and hollering. I ain't heard of anything like that since...since the books of D. L. Moody! It was that kind of stuff. You'd better hope you don't even get close to that kid because he's in a lot of trouble."

I left him and tiptoed up some steps to listen outside the chapel door. I heard the president of the college talking about a "wildfire" young man.

Someone said, "That young man who spoke last night was wildfire! He's Pentecostal, a charismatic! Baptist doctrine doesn't say to beg God and plead for the mighty power of God. Just by faith you claim the baptism of the power of God. If you believe you've got it, then you've got it."

As I listened, I couldn't help but think, "They haven't been reading what I've been reading! They haven't been reading the book of Acts! They haven't been reading that book that Jack Hyles wrote! They haven't been reading John Rice's book on the baptism of the Spirit of God, *The Power of Pentecost*. They haven't been reading Charles Finney's books. They haven't been reading D. L. Moody's sermons. They haven't been reading Peter Cartwright's stories. They haven't been reading the Bible!" In truth, I was deeply disappointed, a little scared, and even a little angry.

The leadership warned my fellow students, "Stay away from him!"

After that service, I went to my room. My roommate came in and said, "You're in trouble! The whole student body just got skinned alive because of you!"

The students obeyed. When I walked down the sidewalk, people would literally turn the other way to avoid me. It was like I had a do-not-enter zone of 50 feet; nobody came near me. One of my roommates wouldn't speak to me. A small handful of peers, including my friend Bob and my senior friend Dave, still did. Most were scared to death to get around me. Almost nobody would talk to me.

I was told that the next few days after the emergency chapel service, 200 phone calls were made to the administrators with the message, "If you let that boy give as much as a testimony again, we'll withdraw our support from your college."

It was like I was branded! I was put on probation and told I could not speak again—not even to give my testimony. I had been preaching for a traveling choir; I no longer had that opportunity. I was the sophomore class chaplain, and I lost the privilege of preaching. I had been preaching out-of-town many weekends, and I lost all of my preaching opportunities.

The faculty members called me a wildfire—a wild kid with Pentecostal wildfire—who would never amount to anything in the ministry. One man looked at me and said, "You are so proud of being humble, you're proudly humble! The arrogance of your sitting in our college and telling us that we need the power of God."

I said, "Sir, I did not say that! I said I need the power of God! I don't know what you need, but I know what I need. I got called to preach by a God Who wants to do something. I don't care what you do, but I know I've got to give account to God some day, and I want a baptism of the Spirit of God."

I was threatened, "You'd better shut your mouth, son. You're in trouble! We'll expel you!"

I said, "Then expel me!"

Mine was not a good attitude to have, but I was tired of being in a school where nobody got anybody saved—except my favorite Bible teacher who won one person to Christ that year! I started a soul-winning ministry that year, and we won 15 to 20 people to Christ every week. Other students and even some faculty members asked me how to win souls.

I wondered, "What am I doing in a college where the faculty members are asking me, a student, how to win souls and where they criticize me because I want the power of God to do it!" I was frustrated and upset! All I knew was that my fire was burning. I knew that what beat in my heart was of God. I didn't want to be a wildfire charismatic. I wanted that mighty baptism of the Spirit of God. I wanted to know what it was like to preach in power; I wanted to know what it was like to win souls in power. I wanted to know what it was like to influence people and see changed lives! I wanted full altars. I wanted baptismal waters stirring! **I wanted God to use a young preacher boy! I was NOT going to be a powerless preacher!**

I went back to those biographies and read them again. I picked up John Wesley's biography and read his words about prayer. He wrote that when he was really busy he would spend an hour with God alone in prayer. When he was really, really busy, he would spend two hours alone with God in prayer, and when he was so busy he couldn't see his way through, he would spend at least three hours with God alone in prayer.

When I read those words, I thought, "God, that's what

I want: I want time with You. I want to walk with You in prayer. I want to know Your mighty power. I want to know what You can do. God, how much can You use me? That's what I want to know."

I continued to beg God to use me, then I transferred to Hyles-Anderson College, and I found other folks like me. The dorms were so full the year I came that two floors of the Holiday Inn in Crete, Illinois, were rented. I was told, "You're going to be in a dormitory 17 miles away from here."

A golf course was being developed there. The paths had been plotted in the woods, and every night I would walk those unfinished paths for about two or three hours. I'd walk through that golf course and pray and beg, "Oh, God! I want something. God, I want something that I can't put my finger on. It's like the night You called me to preach— that's what I want! It's like those stories I read about Charles Finney, D. L. Moody, and John Wesley.

As often as I could, I walked those hills through that golf course, just begging for the power of God. I was transferred to the Schererville campus of Baptist City. Then I walked up and down the streets of Schererville. I'd stay out until the security guards would come and say, "Brother Schaap, you've got to go in the dorms now; it's curfew time."

"I just want to pray," I said.

They said, "We know, but you've got to go inside."

I would go to my room, get in bed and lie there like I was supposed to do. As I'd lie there, I'd say, "Oh, God!" The tears would run down my face. "God, please do something!" I said, "This is a great college with wonderful people, and I love it here. I feel more at home here, but God, I still don't feel social. I still don't like crowds, I still don't know how You are going to use me, but I want to know again and again like that night I got called to preach. I want to know what it's like to be filled again. I want a fresh enduement of power from on high."

Within a month of my transfer to Hyles-Anderson College, the speaking invitations began to come again. I still have no idea where they came from because I have never asked for an opportunity to preach in all the years I have preached. When I asked people where they heard about me, they said, "We just got your name from somewhere. We don't even know who you are. Just come and preach for us."

Some wonderful meetings resulted. I remember preaching in Missouri one night. About 20 minutes into the sermon, a fellow stood up and began to walk the aisle. Then another, and another followed. When I said, "Folks, I haven't given an invitation yet," everybody just stood up and came forward.

I remember standing in the pulpit with tears streaming down my face, and I said, "God, this is what I want. God, if You are going to make me a preacher, I really want to be used of You. God, please use me. God, when I preach, I want something to happen!"

Watching the power of God on the life of Brother Hyles is what drew me to him. Brother Hyles was a man who felt as awkward in crowds as I did. He was a shy and timid man who said he was a little backward, but I realized that here was a man who had a passion for God. Brother Hyles was a man who walked with God, a man who knew that his best Friend was his Boss, God Almighty! Brother Hyles enjoyed being with God more than being with people. When I heard him preach, I would say, "That man has been with the same Person Whom I want to be with."

At this writing, I still feel like the same 17-year-old little boy who got called to preach. Often there seems to be a common thread in preachers. Even though we say we're shy and timid, people never seem to believe us. You didn't know us when we were growing up. If you had asked my sister when she was in grade school, she would have said her brother cried every day because he was so lonely in school. During second grade and third grade, I would sit by the corner of the school building and cry. She would come along and say, "Why are you crying?"

I answered, "I'm lonely, and I don't want to be here. I don't like people, and I'm scared."

I realize I can put a smile on my face and shake hands. I can walk through a crowd on a Sunday morning and shake hands with the people I see in the auditorium class. I can make others feel welcome, but I sit in my office and say to myself, "Come on! You can do it now! Just walk out there and pretend you know what you're doing!"

On Monday I sit in that study and think, "Whoa! We got through another Sunday, God! It was incredible! But, God, we've got to do it again!"

The great secret is getting alone with God in that office and falling on my face and saying, "God, I've got to have it again. I've got to have it again, and again, and again, and again."

If we expect to change America, it will be by a whole lot of God's people falling on their faces and saying, "Oh, God, we need you!"

I say to the men who work with me, "Brother Depper, you cannot run Memory Lane Cemetery without the baptism of the Spirit of God. That's not a business! God's people are buried there. Our church families need a man of God at Memory Lane."

Brother Vogel, you can't run a junior high or conduct an Educators' Convention without the baptism of the Spirit of God. Dr. Evans calls you one of the greatest educators in America. Even with your mind and your talent, as godly and as wonderful as they are, you need that mighty baptism of the Spirit of God. All is vain unless the Spirit of the Living God comes down.

Brother John Francis, you are a very capable man. I can say, "Brother John, we need a thousand people more this week," and you fire up the troops and pass out goldfish! You know that goldfish cannot change people's lives! Having Pumpkin Sunday or Pizza Sunday or Picture Sunday with our promotions doesn't change lives. The baptism of the Spirit of God is what changes lives!

Brother Moffitt, you conduct many soul-winning ministries here at First Baptist Church including the Candle of the Lord Club, the Fishermen's Club, the Truck Stop Ministry, as well as your Sunday school class. Still, you can't change lives unless the Spirit of the Living God comes down.

Brother McKinney, you work with fallen men in the rescue mission and the Homeless Ministry. Those men don't just need a Christian Alcoholics Anonymous. They need more than three square meals a day and a place to sleep. They need a leader filled with the Spirit of God. All is vain unless the Spirit of the Living God comes down.

You lead the choir, Brother Cuozzo, with your talent and experience. You watched Brother Boardway for many years. Those choir members need a director who is filled with the Spirit of God. Choir members, you should fall on your faces before every service and say, "God, use me in that choir! I want to sing as unto the Lord." It doesn't matter whether or not you have a talented voice. All is vain unless the Spirit of the Living God comes down and unless choir members also need to be filled with the Spirit of God.

Brother Colsten visits those in the hospitals and comforts them. He so ably conducts funeral services and comforts the bereaved, but all is in vain unless the Spirit of the Living God comes down.

"Spirit of the Living God, fall fresh on us!" should be our prayer.

Brother Ray Young wrote the book on the bus ministry. He may have conducted Spring and Fall Programs for umpteen times! But, Brother Ray, you need the mighty baptism of the Spirit of God! All is in vain unless the Spirit of the Living God comes down.

Brother Eddie Lapina, you conduct a gigantic Youth Conference every year, and you lead the young people of First Baptist Church. You are confident and comfortable in your role. With your talent and preaching ability, you have the hearts of the teenagers. America loves you! You're America's youth director, but we want those young people's lives changed by the power of God. All is vain unless the Spirit of the Living God comes down.

Brother Bob Marshall, you have been hired to keep Brother Hyles' ministry alive through the printed word, but all is vain unless the Spirit of the Living God comes down.

Brother Sisson, we need that grade school run by a principal and a staff who is baptized in the Spirit of the Living God. Brother Douglass, we need the City Baptist High School baptized in the Spirit of God. Brother Auclair, we need City Baptist Grade School baptized in the Spirit of the Living God. Dr. Evans, we need Hyles-Anderson College baptized in the Spirit of the Living God. With your passion in your heart and your hunger for God, I want you to be an example to those preacher boys and to those young ladies who will love those men who get fired up and love that mighty baptism of God.

We need office workers, assistant pastors, secretaries, custodians, organists, pianists, singers, P.A. men—everybody! We need everybody to beg, "Oh, God! Come down!"

One of the greatest secrets of First Baptist Church of Hammond goes on underneath my feet while I am preaching. A boiler room is under the pulpit area. There are two or three or four men begging and pleading that God will do something special in every service. They pray, "Oh, God! Help our preacher! Oh, God! Help my pastor! Oh, God! Show us Thy mighty power."

We need teenagers to shut off their rock music, to stop trying to emulate the lives of Hollywood's stars, and to get baptized in the Spirit of the Living God. We need moms and dads to stop bickering and fussing and get baptized of the Spirit of God. Some come for marriage counseling, but how many hours do you spend on your face lying prostrate on the floor saying, "Oh, God! Let me be the wife my husband needs!" And "...be the husband my wife needs!" and "...be the parent my kids need!"

Say, "Oh, God! I cannot do it without You! I must have Your power!"

We need deaf people to sign with fingers that are yielded and baptized with the Spirit of God. We need the custodians who keep these buildings clean to fall on their faces and say, "God, I keep Your buildings clean because this is where Your people walk. Oh, God! Baptize me with Your Spirit!"

Young ladies who marry these Hyles-Anderson preacher boys need to feel the mighty baptism of God as they comfort, encourage, and rally their husbands in the hard times and as they stand by their man in the cold, hard days of starting a church. Those who go out to a foreign field need to be baptized in the Spirit of God.

The great secret of First Baptist Church of Hammond is the Spirit of the Living God falling fresh and fresh and fresh and fresh and fresh and fresh on you. If you don't know the mighty power of God on your life, I'm afraid the problem is not with the Giver for the Bible says, *"If ye then, being evil, know how to give good gifts unto your children: how much more shall your heavenly Father give the Holy Spirit to them that ask him?"* (Luke 11:13) The problem is not with the Giver; the problem is with the receiver!

The problem with obtaining that power is that we're so busy. We have all the legitimate excuses. Some people work day and night to make ends meet. I don't even know when you pray, but how do you survive without the Spirit of God? I plead with you to find time to fall on your face and beg God and say, "Oh, God! Spirit of the Living God, fall fresh on me."

CHAPTER TWO

Grieve Not the Holy Spirit

▪   ▪   ▪

"*And grieve not the holy Spirit of God, whereby ye are sealed unto the day of redemption. Let all bitterness, and wrath, and anger, and clamour, and evil speaking, be put away from you, with all malice: And be ye kind one to another, tenderhearted, forgiving one another, even as God for Christ's sake hath forgiven you.*" (Ephesians 4:30-32)

These passages are familiar to most of us. When we were little children, most of us learned a portion of these verses, "*And be ye kind one to another, tenderhearted, forgiving one another....*"

Like many Scriptures we learned, we did not practice them very well or live by them consistently. In this chapter, I want to address a little phrase in verse 30 which has captivated my thinking, "*...grieve not the holy Spirit of God....*"

Perhaps the best way for me to address and explain the matter of grieving the Holy Spirit is for me to relive February 6, 2001, when my father-in-law, Dr. Jack Hyles, went to Heaven. In April of 2001, two months after his Homegoing, I preached a sermon called "How Do I Walk Through the Valley?" In that sermon, I listed 13 stages of grief. These stages were taken largely from the book of

Psalms and primarily from the life of Job about whom 42 chapters are written. Job surely went through a grieving process—losing his children, losing all of his employees except four, losing all of his money, losing all of his wealth, losing most of his earthly belongings, and losing the respect and admiration of his own family and loved ones.

The 13 stages of grief about which I spoke are very important to the content of this chapter. I want to list those 13 stages of grief with brief explanations then use them as a pivotal point to teach a matter of great importance for every Christian's life.

1. **A divine approval of the painful plan.** Nothing comes our way without first being approved by God. *"And the LORD said unto Satan, Behold, all that he hath is in thy power; only upon himself put not forth thine hand. So Satan went forth from the presence of the LORD."* (Job 1:12)

2. **Automatic response.** We humans experience a natural "knee-jerk" reaction when the negative circumstances enter our lives. What you have been becoming now exposes itself. Job feared God. *"There was a man in the land of Uz, whose name was Job; and that man was perfect and upright, and one that feared God, and eschewed evil."* (Job 1:1) Job's initial automatic response is to worship God, *"Then Job arose, and rent his mantle, and shaved his head, and fell down upon the ground, and worshipped."* (Job 1:20)

3. **Numbness.** Our emotions become paralyzed, and we feel as though we are living in another dimension. Often this stage is referred to as "clinical depression." *"So they sat down with him upon the ground seven days and seven nights, and none spake a word unto him: for they saw that his grief was very great."* (Job 2:13)

4. **Searching.** In our grief, we begin searching for reasons, for someone to understand, for comfort, and for relief from the pain. If you read Job chapter three, you will notice

the "whys" expressed by Job in verses 11, 12, 20, and 23.

5. **Anger.** *"My soul is weary of my life; I will leave my complaint upon myself; I will speak in the bitterness of my soul. I will say unto God, Do not condemn me; shew me wherefore thou contendest with me."* (Job 10:1, 2)

6. **Guilt.** In Job 7: 20 and 21, Job cries out that he has sinned. He begins to blame himself for the problems that have assaulted him and his wife. This guilt is a very real problem with those who have suffered great tragedy. There is a strong tendency to blame one's self for the loss of another person and to even feel guilty that he is alive or healthy while his loved one is ill or dead. "It should have been I who suffered the pain or who should have died," is often the human cry of grief at this stage.

7. **Self-neglect.** Personal neglect of basic hygiene or appearance is common. As one widow said sadly to me, "There's no reason for me to get dressed up anymore. There's no one to notice or compliment me if I do." *"My breath is corrupt, my days are extinct, the graves are ready for me."* (Job 17:1)

8. **Self-pity.** The entire nineteenth chapter of Job reveals Job's feeling very alone and very sorry for himself. Notice especially verses 13-19, *"He hath put my brethren far from me, and mine acquaintance are verily estranged from me. My kinsfolk have failed, and my familiar friends have forgotten me. They that dwell in mine house, and my maids, count me for a stranger: I am an alien in their sight. I called my servant, and he gave me no answer; I intreated him with my mouth. My breath is strange to my wife, though I intreated for the children's sake of mine own body. Yea, young children despised me; I arose, and they spake against me. All my inward friends abhorred me: and they whom I loved are turned against me."*

9. **Self-righteousness.** This stage is dangerous because it is where the grieving person often begins to justify

certain injustices or indiscretions. *"So these three men ceased to answer Job, because he was righteous in his own eyes."* (Job 32:1)

10. **Humbling.** Job is humbled by his experience. He has been rebuked by God, and now he is responding in Job 42:1-6. Notice especially the great humility of verse 6, *"Wherefore I abhor myself, and repent in dust and ashes."*

11. **Renewed awareness of God.** Suffering and grieving can darken the spiritual understanding of a person or awaken his spiritual perception. *"I have heard of thee by the hearing of the ear: but now mine eye seeth thee."* (Job 42:5)

12. **Renewed desire to help others.** Job now looks about him and sees that in spite of his own hurt and grief, his friends have not learned the great lessons of life that he has learned. There is no gloating or pride or self-pity; there is the honest desire to help those less fortunate than he. This desire should always be a key manifestation of suffering **in** the will of God. *"And the LORD turned the captivity of Job, when he prayed for his friends...."* (Job 42:10)

13. **Renewed productivity for God.** Again in Job 42:10, Job is looking for those he can help. Notice, he was not yet delivered from his affliction. In his affliction Job began helping others, then God began using him and increasing his influence. It was only after Job prayed for his friends that Job began to thoroughly heal.

Why is mentioning these 13 stages so important to this chapter? Since February 6, 2001, the people of the First Baptist Church of Hammond have gone through many cycles of grieving. For instance, when my dad called to talk with me, in the course of our conversation, I said, "Dad, I think that with all I've gone through in the year 2001, I doubt if my getting Alzheimer's disease could cause me to forget the year 2001. Too many big events have happened, and those events are staggering."

Our church went through just cycle after cycle of grieving with the Homegoing of Brother Hyles. Just five months later Marlene Evans, the founder of *Christian Womanhood*, passed away. The church people were saying, "I'm still not able to focus clearly on what has happened since the loss of our pastor, Brother Hyles."

Six months after the Homegoing of Brother Hyles, a staff member who has talked to me by the hour said, "I don't understand me. I feel like I should be jumping on board and being one of the leaders of the pack in all these new ministries being started at the church. I need you to scold me and chasten me. Just tell me that I'm really backslidden and that I need to get right with God because I just feel numb. I can't get out of that grieving stage. What's wrong with me? Do you think I'll ever recover?"

I thought of my dear wife who said, "I get up sometimes in the middle of the night just to cry because the loss of my dad hurts so badly. I have had to decide between showing on my face the pain of losing my dad and showing the joy that my husband is the pastor of the church. When I feel that I have to make that decision, I hear Dad's voice echoing, 'Cindy, don't fail at being a good wife.' So I put on a smile of joy for my husband, rather than reveal the grief and pain I feel because of losing my dad."

For nearly a year, during the 6:00 hour on Sunday nights, different people were chosen to share ways they remembered Brother Hyles. Many of our church members came only for the 7:00 service. They were not yet ready to remember Brother Hyles in a certain way.

I am often amazed at the insight of children and teenagers. A 16-year-old boy remarked to me, "Brother Schaap, I just keep waiting for Brother Hyles to walk out the auditorium door like he always did. It's been over six months, and I just now realized that he's never walking out of that door again."

I have had many tell me that they cannot listen to the audio sermons or watch the videotaped sermons of Brother Hyles' preaching. They feel backslidden because they have not listened to his tapes. The reason they are not listening to his tapes is because of the pain of hearing his one-of-a-kind voice which preached over 50,000 sermons. Nobody had a voice like his, but that voice is silenced now except for his tapes and videos. Looking at those tape titles brings back a whole flood of memories because you remember a certain sermon with his illustrations or because the title makes you think of how Brother Hyles taught about certain subjects. Those poignant memories take you back through each of those 13 stages of grieving all over again.

Paul's statement, *"...grieve not the holy Spirit...,"* has taken on a whole different meaning to me as I hear from those who still grieve the memory of Brother Hyles. May I say that how First Baptist Church members feel about the loss of their pastor is exactly how the Spirit of God feels when you cause Him grief?

I do not want to bring deity down to humanity; I want to raise humanity up to understand that deity and humanity are not separated by a great gulf. We are made in His image. Our emotions and our feelings were given to us by a God Who has those same emotions and feelings.

Have you ever thought that the tears you weep were given to you by a God Who knows what tears are? The Bible says He puts all your tears in a bottle and keeps them. They are very important and very precious to Him. John 11:35 says, *"Jesus wept."* The God Who can weep invented tears!

Because deity weeps, humans weep. You feel emotional pain in your soul at the loss of someone you loved more than life because that emotion came from the God Who loves more than life. The feelings of loss, of emptiness, of pain, of sorrow, of sadness, of numbness, of bewilderment, of confusion, of loneliness, of frustration, of anger, of disappointment, and of disillusionment are not sinful emotions. It is not a sin to be disappointed, nor is it a sin to feel pain. It is not necessarily a sin to be angry because the Bible says, *"Be ye angry, and sin not."* (Ephesians 4:26a) On earth, Jesus was angry many times. In Psalm 89:46, the Bible says, *"How long, LORD? wilt thou hide thyself for ever? shall thy wrath burn like fire?"* Wrath is not sinful in itself because God is a God of wrath. The emotions of numbness and emptiness that a grieving person feels come from the God Who gave those feelings to him.

When I hear people say, "I'm not ready to see certain pictures of Brother Hyles," or "I'm not ready to listen to a certain tape," or "I'm not ready to go to the mausoleum," I realize those people are still grieving the loss of a great man of God. Is it sinful? Oh, no! It is grief that has prevented a person from listening to a tape or visiting the mausoleum or looking at pictures.

When my wife rises at night, goes downstairs to our family room, and weeps over the loss of her hero-dad, is she wrong? Oh, no! She's grieving.

That same pain, that same grief, and that same sorrow is exactly what the Spirit of the Living God feels when we grieve the Holy Spirit. We hurt Him to the point where the Spirit of God says, "I don't want to look at that any more."

When we rise on Saturday morning, we say, "Holy Spirit, let's go to the bus route now."

He responds, "I'm not ready for it."

"You're not ready for it? You're the Spirit of the Living God."

"Sorry, I just don't feel like it," the Spirit replies.

"But, Holy Spirit, let's knock on doors and tell people about Jesus."

"You go ahead; I don't feel like it."

Can you imagine the Holy Spirit not feeling like calling on a church bus route or not wanting to read the Words He wrote? That is like a person grieving over the loss of Brother Hyles as his pastor and saying, "I haven't played one of his tapes yet."

About six months following the Homegoing of Brother Hyles, I played a music CD with a narration piece on it by Brother Hyles. I put my head in my hands, and the tears ran between my fingers. I said, "God, I miss him. God, I miss him. I really miss him." Sometimes I turn off the lights in what was his office, lie down on my face, and say, "God, what am I doing in Brother Hyles' study? Why am I here? I don't feel like preparing a sermon today. I don't want to hear a sermon tape by Brother Hyles or hear his voice and remember."

Do I not want to remember Brother Hyles because I don't love Brother Hyles? NO! Sometimes it hurts me too much to remember him, and that is exactly how the Holy Spirit feels when He is grieved.

Christians, at times you wonder why you feel the way you do, when the Holy Spirit retreats into the farthest recess of your spirit. He goes as far as He can—back into the deep, dark depths, just like my wife runs to the basement, closes the door, and weeps tears of pain. Sometimes she begs, "Oh, God, help me! I miss my dad! I loved him so much. I miss him."

The Spirit of God runs to the darkened recesses of your life and says, "I just want to cry. I'm grieved! I'm hurt and sad!"

You ask, "The Spirit of God really does that?"

Yes! Christians grieve the Holy Spirit. At times, He feels abandoned and lost! Sometimes He says, "I don't want to read right now with you."

At those times, when you read your Bible, you say, "I don't get anything out of it."

The Spirit of God says, "I'm sorry. Maybe you should just scold me. I'm living inside of you, and I'm supposed to make that Book come alive. I'm just kind of numb right now."

Just as an individual going through the stages of grieving and hurting, and taking that automatic response and just keeps walking, the Holy Spirit moves inside of a person. When His Spirit is wounded, He hurts. When you grieve Him, the Spirit takes that blow and says, "I don't believe it! He's one of My children! Why did he do that?"

For a while, the Spirit of God suffers through the various emotions. That's why, so often after a person has sinned, he can keep on going and everything seems fine. He can say, "I read my Bible, pray, and everything is fine," because the Holy Spirit is on, what I call, automatic pilot for a while. That is also why so many Christians who sin and backslide ignore a warning such as, "Watch it! You're living dangerously."

The person merely says, "Oh, I'm doing fine," because the Holy Spirit is still on automatic pilot, but then He becomes numb with the pain caused by the sin and the resulting grief that sets in followed by bewilderment and confusion.

You ask, "The Holy Spirit gets bewildered and confused?"

Let me ask some questions. "Where do you think you learned how to grieve? Where do you think you learned how to stand the hurt and go through the grieving process? How do you know Job wasn't just acting out how God felt because Job treated Him that way?"

Christians tend to see themselves as separated by such a huge gulf between God and themselves. To some, God is an old Man up in Heaven with a long, white beard Who sprinkles spoofle dust and Who bonks angels on the head with a golden rod. Too many Christians have a warped idea of Who God is.

The truth is, He has taken His own Spirit and put that Spirit with all of the emotions of love and sorrow inside of every Christian. As a result, man can experience all the feelings that come from God. All of the emotions a person has in his body, sorrow, sadness, tears, love, and grief, come from God. If a person can grieve, so can God because the Bible says that we can grieve the Spirit of God.

When Brother Hyles went to Heaven, I believe God said, "Just like those people are grieving the loss of their beloved pastor right now, I'm grieving, too."

When Marlene Evans went to Heaven in July and people grieved, I believe God said, "I feel that same way."

Brother Hyles' passing did not grieve the Holy Spirit. The Bible says, *"Precious in the sight of the LORD is the death of his saints."* (Psalm 116:15) He is pleased. Brother Hyles is getting to spend a lot of time with God now. I believe God is very pleased to have Brother Hyles with Him. However, the grief of the Holy Spirit is something a child of God causes Him. That is why so often, as Christians, we wonder why we feel a certain way. Perhaps we have a grieving Holy Spirit inside.

The person who caused the Holy Spirit to grieve can make excuses like, "I did that sin a long time ago; He should have gotten over it."

Let me ask a question: "Are you over the Homegoing of Brother Hyles?" Saying, "Well, He's God, and He can get over it," doesn't cure a grieving Holy Spirit. You are made in His image! I don't say to the person who speaks of grieving over Brother Hyles, "Aren't you over Brother Hyles yet? It's been almost six months or one year or even two years!"

I don't say to my wife, "Just grow up and get over it! After all, he's in Heaven with Jesus."

Of course, I wouldn't make such statements, but we treat God that way. We expect God to put up with our sins, put up with our stupidity, put up with our foolishness, and put up with that which grieves Him. We can hurt Him deeply! We wound His Spirit, and He says, "I'm broken. I don't feel like doing My work right now. The problem isn't that I don't love you; I just don't want to talk to you from My Word right now. You hurt Me."

How Do We Grieve the Holy Spirit?

Ephesians 4:31 and 32 say, *"Let all bitterness, and wrath, and anger, and clamour, and evil speaking, be put away from you with all malice: And be ye kind one to another, tenderhearted, forgiving one another...."* The number one way we grieve the Holy Spirit is in how we treat other Christians. I believe the Christians we hurt the most are ones with whom we live. Many times the way husbands and wives talk to each other is so hurtful. The way parents talk to their children is so hurtful. The unkind tongue, the sharp words, the rebellious attitude that teenagers give to their parents is so hurtful. When the Spirit of God hears that hurtful talk, He is wounded, grieved, and pained. Numbness and confusion result. Perhaps you wonder why Christian teenagers just don't seem to catch it sometimes. The Spirit of God has been paralyzed in their lives because He is broken with grief. He is crying out in anguish and tears.

I believe we have such a high depression rate among Christian people because we have broken the spirit of the Holy Spirit. We have brought grief and pain to God's Spirit, and we walk around depressed and saying, "I just don't feel good." Then to cope, we insult Him even more by taking drugs and trying to find some kind of artificial stimulant to boost our spirits or to calm our spirits. Some take amphetamines to get up and tranquilizers to calm down; if that is not enough, they use sleeping pills or other prescriptions.

When children and young people rebel against their parents, the parents rush to doctors, and the children are diagnosed with A.D.D., and Ritalin is prescribed. Ritalin is not what that young person needs!

The Spirit of God living inside of him says, "I am grieved at how you talk to your parents!" The Spirit has been grieved! A teen listens to rock music which invites Hell into his own soul. Then he wonders why there is no victory in his life.

The Spirit of God says, "I'm numb! I don't feel like I can work! I feel so hurt."

That teenager has the very power of God in his life. He has crippled the power of God by grieving the agent—the Holy Spirit. How can you listen to that Satanic music and wonder why you have no victory, teenager?

God says, "I just want to go away and cry! I just want to descend into the basement of your spirit. I want to weep in sadness. I hurt!"

When the Spirit of God is grieved, there is no victory or joy! That's why a Christian has to find artificial stimulation through drugs. That's why a Christian will sneak around and get the stimulation of sexuality to become motivated again. That Christian's spirit is dead inside of him! He has broken the Holy Spirit's heart!

How Do We Ignore the Holy Spirit?

We continuously ignore the Book. Instead of reading the Bible, we continuously watch video after video. As a result, we grieve the Holy Spirit. It is no wonder He doesn't want to speak to us when we read our token two or three chapters on Sunday morning in order to feel like we did something spiritual. It's no wonder He doesn't want to speak to those who would rather read the *Reader's Digest* or a sports magazine or the sports section of the daily newspaper.

God says, "You wonder why you don't have victory? Because you have grieved Me!"

The Holy Spirit Who lives inside of you experiences the same emotions, the same feelings, the same pain, the same loss, the same suffering, the same anguish, the same numbness, the same anger, the same clamor, the same confusion, and the same bewilderment as you do. That is why you feel the way you do!

I preached a message from Romans 8:28 before I became pastor of First Baptist Church of Hammond. In that sermon I said, "I am in no rush to get over the grieving process." I have even told Dr. Ray Young, the Co-President of Hyles-Anderson College, "Brother Ray, I think you ought to take the next 20 to 30 years to grieve over Brother Hyles. Apart from your wife and children, he was the closest person in the world to you."

For some of you who have grieved the Spirit of God, it will take months of right living before you and the Holy Spirit are able to walk arm in arm again. Until then, you will stagger along and say, "I think we are going to be okay."

This business of Christianity is long-term, day after day after day. If you wound your wife's spirit, you can get forgiveness. Still, you and I both know it takes days and sometimes weeks before the trust is restored. Keep wounding her spirit, 15 or 20 or 30 times, and it will be years before the trust is fully restored again because she is grieving. That process of grief is as sure and certain for the Spirit of God as it is for you.

[49]

How Do We Grieve the Holy Spirit?

We grieve Him by not investing or inviting His influence into our lives. When I preach without inviting the Spirit of God to help me, or when you play that piano without inviting the Spirit of God to help you or when you sing without inviting the Spirit of God to help you or when you lead singing without inviting the Spirit of God to help you or when you lead a church bus route without inviting the Spirit of God to help you or when you teach in a school without inviting the Spirit of God to help you or when you run your place of business such as Hyles Publications without inviting the Spirit of God to help you, He is grieved. Whenever you do anything without pleading and begging and inviting the leadership of God and without acknowledging the presence of God, you wound His Spirit and grieve the Holy Spirit of God.

He says, "I was sent to do that for you. I was sent to help you! I was sent to give you the mind of Christ to lead you! Acknowledge Me!"

Instead, many ignore Him and continue to ignore Him. Some go for years ignoring the Holy Spirit. You have operated in the only energy you know—the energy of your own creative mind and the energy of your flesh. As a result, you have hurt and wounded the Spirit of the Living God. That is exactly why you are not seeing the victory you want to see.

How Do We Grieve the Holy Spirit?

We grieve Him by the way we treat fellow human beings. Ephesians 4:32 says, *"And be ye kind...."*

[50]

It is amazing what you learn when you become pastor of a church. It is amazing to me how some people who have been saved for so long, who know so much Bible, and who have sat for so many years under the influence of Brother Hyles cannot get along with each other. The knowledge that I have had to call some into my office several times and say, "Please, I beg of you! I plead with you to get along with your co-workers!" staggers my mind.

I cannot help but think, "Have you heard anything Brother Hyles taught?" I believe a part of the problem is that the Holy Spirit has been grieved for many years. He has been paralyzed in some people's lives. As a result, He cannot work. It's not that He doesn't want to work; He just grieves! I believe in some cases, He weeps every night.

When I pleaded with some workers, one response I received was, "Well, I'll just quit then."

I did not call in that person to ask for a resignation. I called in that person to say, "Why don't you and the Holy Spirit of God get along with each other? Please make peace with the Spirit of God and humble yourself. You need to say, 'Spirit of the Living God, I am so sorry. How in the world could I have done this to You?' "

When Brother Hyles went to Heaven, some people, in their grief, quit speaking to the Holy Spirit. They were trying to get through their grief and have grieved the Comforter. How are you going to receive comfort, which is the job of the Comforter, when you ignore and hurt Him? You don't speak to Him. You don't yield to Him. You don't acknowledge Him. You don't talk to Him! If your marriage were like that, you would have been served with divorce papers!

I have marveled at parents who have available to them the wisdom of a Dr. Don Boyd, a Dr. Tom Vogel, a Dr. Mike Sisson, a Dr. Dave Douglass, as well as the wisdom of many

[51]

counselors who are experts in their chosen fields, but they still do not know how to capture the heart of their teen. Many have sought counsel, have studied and read their books, and have heard preaching on the subject, but they still do not know how to win the hearts of their children. I am staggered at that thought! Do you not know how to say to your teenage son, "I love you, buddy"? Do you not know how to knock on his door, walk into his room, and say, "Good night, son; I love you pal"? Can it be that difficult to show love to those flesh and blood children who call you mom and dad?

Possibly the reason why you cannot improve upon that parent-teenager or parent-child relationship is because you have paralyzed the Spirit of God for so many months and years that He is totally grieved. You don't tiptoe to their rooms. If you did, instead of seeing your young person, you would see something that you did not like. Perhaps you see a pile of underwear on the floor. You see clothes that aren't put away. You see a poster on the wall that you do not like. Instead of speaking love, you rip and snort about all that you do not like, and the kids say, "Yeah, I hear you." Parent, you have havoc in your home because you have grieved the Holy Spirit!

Do you want that fresh anointing of the Holy Spirit? Do you want that breath of power on your ministry? Do you want to preach and to see souls get saved and to see lives being changed? Do you want to build a bus route and to see souls saved? Do you want to see your converts being baptized? Do you want your Sunday school class to grow? Do you want to see your marriage flourish? Do you want to be a productive, fruit-bearing Christian? You cannot without the Spirit of the Living God. When you grieve the Holy Spirit, you have removed all the power you need to make a difference. Anything you can humanly do is vain except for the Spirit of the Living One inside of you doing His work. However, He is not going to do His work if we have grieved Him because He is paralyzed with the pain, the hurt, the sadness, and the numbness of being ignored, of being refused, of not even being spoken to, of our insulting other Christians, and of our trying to do His work without Him.

How Do We Grieve the Holy Spirit?

We grieve the Holy Spirit when we are ungrateful. Nothing hurts the Spirit of God more than after He has worked, for us not to acknowledge His role.

I read about the man, Charles G. Finney. After reading Finney's biography, I sought and sought and sought and sought Holy Spirit power. Why did that man have such incredible power? Several years after his revival campaigns, researchers carefully analyzed his meetings, spoke to his converts, and learned that 92 percent to 95 percent of his converts still attended prayer meeting ten years later.

When I read those statistics, I asked, "God, how did that happen?"

I stumbled across a statement made by Charles Finney that I believe gave me the answer. "When God uses me in a great way, I always spend a minimum of three hours after the service, thanking God for how good He was."

Suppose I called a young preacher out in the ministry and said, "I want you to preach to 5,000 teenagers at the annual Youth Conference at First Baptist Church of Hammond."

Instead of calling all of your friends to say, "You won't believe it, but I got called to speak at the Youth Conference at First Baptist Church of Hammond," you ought to fall on your face and beg and plead, "Oh, God, use me. Oh, God, use me. Oh, God, use me!"

That young preacher would have probably cleaned up his act. He would have gone through every magazine and book in his library to be sure it was decent and said, "Oh, God, I've got to have Your power. Oh, God, give me Your power."

"How do you know that's what he would do?" Because that is exactly what I would have done!

Then if God would have met with that young man, he would have signed Bibles, perhaps been offered opportunities to preach at other churches because of the incredible job he did, remade the old letterhead with his name, and perhaps produced a flier or brochure with his picture on it. After all was said and done, God might have received a token, "Oh, by the way, thanks, God!" But would God hear you praise Him after the great meeting as much as He heard you beg Him before the meeting?

I decided a long time ago when I read that statement by Charles Finney that God was going to hear from me at least as much afterward as He did beforehand. "Thank You, God! Thank You, God! Thank You, God" was going to be a great part of my vocabulary.

At the first Youth Conference after Brother Hyles went to Heaven, I walked onto the platform and saw a jam-packed auditorium. Brother Eddie said, "Brother Schaap, the church has never been this full in the history of Youth Conference."

Later that evening, I rushed back to my office, fell on my face, and said, "Oh, God, thank You! Thank You! Thank You! Thank You! Ten thousand times, thank You! To God be the glory!"

Do you thank Him for the big days on the bus routes? Do you thank Him for the times He moves in that wonderful way you desire? "To God be the glory! Thank You,

Lord!" At that Youth Conference, 576 teenage boys and young men came to the platform and said in a microphone, "I'm going to make a difference." As they reached the microphone, some would holler and scream a statement like, "My name is (so and so), and I'm going to make a 255,000-degree difference!" We even had to move along a couple of young men because they got to preaching!

I returned to my office after that wonderful service and said, "Oh, God, thank You! Thank You! Thank You! Thank You! Ten thousand times, thank You! Thank You! Thank You! Thank You!" I don't ever want to forget the One Who honored the prayers before the service by neglecting him after the service.

Let First Baptist Church of Hammond be the most grateful church that God has in all of His kingdom. Let the First Baptist Church members be the ones who make God say, "I've got to use First Baptist Church because you won't believe how they praise Me when I bless them." Let God be so wanting to bless us because we are so grateful for what He does for us.

When the baptistery waters stir, we need to say, "Thank You, Jesus!" When the aisles are filled and converts are saved and baptized, we need to say, "Thank You, Jesus." It is not just a matter of taking it for granted; it is a matter of expressing our love and gratitude. Nothing hurts the Spirit of God more than when He does move and does work, and we don't fall on our faces and say, "Thank You! To God be the glory! Great things You have done! Oh, thank You, God! Thank You! Thank You! Thank You! Ten thousand times, thank You! Thank You! Thank You! Thank You! Oh, God, thank You."

When He gives you the power for which you have pleaded, do you thank Him like you begged for His power? The power is found as much in the gratitude you display afterward as it is in the pleading beforehand.

God knows too many of what I call "foxhole pleadings." When the pressure is on, people beg, "Oh, God, please come through," but after the pressure is over, they say, "I'm the man!"

At a person's best stage, he's altogether vanity! We're just sinners saved by the grace of God. To God be the glory! To God be the glory! To God be the glory! Lift Him up! He came to seek and to save the lost, and He gives us His power. He alone can save. No man comes to Christ except the Father draws him. If a person received Christ, it wasn't because of another person's soul-winning prowess and skill! That person was saved because of the power of the Living God!

When you start thinking, "I work so hard for Jesus; I've done a lot of things," Jesus says, "Remember, I served it all at Calvary. Remember, it's My Spirit that you grieve."

How Do We Grieve the Holy Spirit?

We grieve the Holy Spirit when we hinder other spirit-filled Christians. Criticism grieves the Holy Spirit.

Since becoming pastor of First Baptist Church of Hammond, I have had a real revelation about how petty some very good friends of mine have been about my becoming pastor. Letters have been circulating where the writers called me unworthy of the position. Others have stated, "Who does Schaap think he is?" or "What's he trying to do—become the next 'king of fundamentalism'?"

Yes, I am unworthy, and no, I am not trying to become the next king. I just want to be a servant. I am not angry about these criticisms. For me to become angry would grieve the Spirit. I did not seek the pastorate of First Baptist

Church of Hammond. Never in over 27 years of preaching have I ever asked one time for a speaking engagement. If God is not a big enough God to hire me and keep me employed, He's not a very big God.

Years ago, one of our graduates who was totally out of control called me. He said, "Oh, Brother Schaap, I'm so glad I got in touch with you. I am in trouble. A petition is being passed around church to vote me out."

When my only comment was, "So?" he said, "What do I do?"

I said, "You don't want to stay someplace where you are not wanted. Probably you want to go more than they want you to go."

"Well, yes," he agreed, "but that's not the point."

"What's the point?"

He said, "They are making up lies about me."

When I asked, "What are they lying about?" he shared three ridiculous arguments. One involved his purchasing some paint to paint a couple of chairs. He used the leftover paint at his house, and the members thought it was a misappropriation of funds. He had put a lock on his study door without the approval of the deacons. The other charge involved a sign.

After listening to his story, I gave him the following advice: "Here's what you do. Can you think of 97 other things about you that you don't like about yourself?"

"Oh, I can think of 100 of them," he maintained.

"Wonderful. They don't know those yet, do they?"

He laughed and said, "No."

"Sign the petition that you want the pastor to leave, and list at the bottom the 97 things you don't like about yourself of which they are ignorant. Go to church with your signed petition and a big smile on your face. Walk in happy and start laughing as soon as you get behind the pulpit. Say,

'Folks, you are looking at the happiest pastor in the whole world tonight.' "

He argued, "But I'm not happy!"

I said, "Fake it!"

"Why should I be happy?"

I said, "Because you know 97 things about you that they have not yet discovered!"

That graduate is still pastoring that church. Use that example as a reminder to not get upset with people who do not like the way you do something. The truth of the matter is, if people knew the truth about any of us, our friends would abandon us. Getting upset with fellow Christians grieves the Holy Spirit of God.

Let me ask you a question. "At your worst moments, what kind of a Christian are you?" Aren't you glad that only the Holy Spirit of God knows the real truth? That's why He questions, "Why do you get so upset when people fabricate a lie? I know more about you than any critic knows!" When a person gets so upset about a fabrication, he wounds the Spirit and paralyzes the work of the Spirit. Basically I am saying that the same pain and grief and sorrow and numbness and confusion and lack of desire to get motivated to do God's work that you feel is because you are grieving the loss of a loved one who has died is the same emotional struggle that the Holy Spirit of God feels inside of you when you bring grief to Him. That's why you do not have the victory you want! That's why you do not have the productivity you desire! That's why you don't have the joy you want. When you have grieved the Holy Spirit, you will not get over it quickly, just as our church will not get over the loss of Brother Hyles quickly. Repairs begin when a Christian humbles himself at an old-fashioned altar.

CHAPTER THREE

How to Be Filled with the Holy Spirit

◼   ◼   ◼

Hyles-Anderson College is a Baptist college owned and operated by the First Baptist Church of Hammond, Indiana. The Board of Deacons at First Baptist Church is the Board of Directors of Hyles-Anderson College. Our college is an independent, fundamental, Baptist college. We advertise that, and everybody knows that. We do allow students from different denominations to attend our school; however, every student who is from another denomination is instructed by our Admissions Office that we are a Baptist school, and we make sure they understand that. Every so often we'll have somebody come in who is from a non-Baptist background who thinks they understand that we are an independent Baptist college, but don't, and they feel it's their God-given duty to teach their non-Baptist doctrine. Once in a while I believe it is wise, as the Chancellor of our college and Pastor of the church that owns this college, to take a little time and address this issue and make sure we're all on the same page.

We're a practical school here. Brother Hyles often

taught, "If I read a truth in the Bible, and I can't do something with it; then it's not practical to me, and I don't care to learn that truth that deeply. It's not something I really want to know." In other words, he didn't really care to learn truth that he couldn't live. Brother Hyles was not interested in just learning for the sake of filling his mind with facts or information. Like Brothers Hyles, I'm interested in learning truth so I can live it. I am a living human being. I'm not just a library or a reservoir of information. I want to use what I have learned. To me, this experience of life is the most amazing thing in the world. and if I cannot live the truths I find, they are impractical. In my thinking, there's not a whole lot of sense in cluttering up the areas in my mind that I could be filling with practical truths. With that in mind, I want to address this matter of being filled with the Spirit. This is not a deep, theological study, but a very practical study.

I'll be honest with you young preachers: all of you must learn to preach practically and preach where the average layman lives—the man who drives a truck or tightens a wrench around a pipe or swings a hammer to build a house or works in a factory. If he cannot use that truth in the factory or behind the wheel of a truck or in the office space or on the construction site or use it in his home, there's not much sense in your teaching such truths. I want to live the truths that I've learned, so I want to preach practical truths. Preachers, don't try to impress your people with how much you've learned; instead, impress them with how practical you've become and how helpful you've become.

Ephesians 5:18 states, *"And be not drunk with wine, wherein is excess; but be filled with the Spirit."* Allow me to teach you a little bit of English, a little bit of Bible, and a lot of practical truth in this chapter. In the verse, *"And be not drunk with wine, wherein is excess;"* notice the punctuation mark right after the word, *excess*. It is a semi-colon. The verse continues, *"but be filled with the Spirit; Speaking to yourselves in psalms and hymns and spiritual songs, singing and making melody in your heart to the Lord;..."* Again the punctuation is a semi-colon. In the next verse, *"Giving thanks always for all things unto God and the Father in the name of our Lord Jesus Christ;"* the punctuation again was a semi-colon. The thought is concluded in verse 21 with, *"Submitting yourselves one to another in the fear of God."* A period, of course, is the last punctuation mark. That means every word in verse 18, beginning with *And,* and continuing to the end of verse 21 with the word *God,* is all one thought. These verses are one thought building on another and explaining a little more thoroughly; it's almost like building blocks.

I know the word *And,* connects verse 18 to the previous verses, but I just want to talk about the part of the chapter dealing with being filled with the Holy Spirit of God.

"And be not drunk with wine, wherein is excess...." The word *excess* means "going outside the boundaries." When a person exceeds the speed limit, he goes outside the boundaries of the speed limit. When a person lives a life of excess, he is going outside of the boundaries of what God taught. Ephesians 5:1-17 explains the boundaries.

For instance, Ephesians 5:1-4 says, *"Be ye therefore followers of God, as dear children; And walk in love, as Christ also hath loved us, and hath given himself for us an offering and a sacrifice to God for a sweetsmelling savour. But fornication, and all uncleanness, or covetousness, let it not be once named among you, as becometh saints; Neither filthiness, nor foolish talking, nor jesting, which are not convenient: but rather giving of thanks."* These verses teach the boundary of not even talking about fornication; don't let it even be named among you. Fornication encompasses reading pornography, sleeping with someone who is not your spouse, lewdness, indecent behavior, adultery, and every other form of moral and sexual perversion. More specifically it means an unmarried couple sleeping together, but it also includes all sexual sins.

God is saying He doesn't even want the subject brought up in casual conversation. Don't joke or jest about it. Don't call each other homosexuals as a joke. Don't even say that your brother's a sodomite in jest. God was saying that those subjects are so distasteful in His mind that He didn't even want people to go there.

All the rest of the verses in this passage are also addressing this kind of behavior. Verse 12 says, *"For it is a shame even to speak of those things which are done of them in secret."* Ephesians 5:1-17 is saying to let your walk and your talk be so aboveboard that there's no hint of anything immoral either in your lifestyle or your language. These verses are just a background summary for verses 18-21. *"And be not drunk with wine, wherein is excess."* God was saying, "Don't let anything possess you that would give you license or freedom to exceed those boundaries of immoral behavior." In other words, a dating couple might justify fornicating if they get drunk. The word *drunkenness* is the word, *debauchery.* It is the idea of a life lived which has been artificially stimulated by external sources. God was saying, "Don't let anything come into your life that will seemingly allow you permission to break down your defenses to where you start living a life outside of the right boundaries." Instead, stay well inside the proper boundaries and be motivated from the inside by being filled with the Spirit of God.

What does it mean to be filled with the Spirit of God? The Bible says in Ephesians 5:18a, *"And be not drunk with wine, wherein is excess."* Those first 17 verses teach us about some things not to exceed. They list some of the boundaries. Don't let your body exceed what it should not do; rather, be filled with the Holy Spirit. Notice the semi-colon after the word *excess*. The way to not exceed the boundaries of God's laws is to be filled with the Spirit.

You ask, "What does that semi-colon mean?" That punctuation mark tells you how to be filled with the Holy Spirit of God. It tells the reader that the next words will explain what he just read. God is saying, "Keep reading, and I'll explain how you can be filled with the Spirit." Allow me to paraphrase this passage: "Don't allow wine or other kinds of sinful habits to break down your will power to do right and to stay within the boundaries of God's laws. How can you stay within the boundaries? Be filled with the Holy Spirit. How can you be filled with the Holy Spirit? Speak to yourselves in psalms and hymns and spiritual songs...."

Let's examine this simple formula for being filled with the Holy Spirit. This is intensely practical. Learn it well, and you will understand how you can be filled with God's Spirit anytime you desire.

1. **"Speaking to yourselves in psalms and hymns and spiritual songs."** These are the words found in Ephesians 5:19 following the semi-colon at the end of verse 18. God is telling us that this is how you begin to be filled with His Spirit.

God tells us to "speak" to ourselves. Certainly, it is proper to sing these songs, but God is teaching us the importance of the words of these psalms, hymns, and spiritual songs; thus, God commands us to speak these songs to ourselves. God is not referring here to congregational singing in church but to personal speaking in private.

The word *psalms* is listed first. Why? Because God wrote 150 of them for us to use as the beginning point of being filled with His Spirit. Open up your Bible to Psalms each morning and start your day off right by reading a Psalm out loud to yourself.

The word *hymns* refers to those songs that praise God for

[63]

His character and qualities. Songs like "Great Is Thy Faithfulness" and "To God Be the Glory" are examples of great hymns. Get a songbook and open it each day to read one or more hymns from it. Don't start singing them yet; just read the words, and notice how your heart and spirit begin to perk up.

Spiritual songs are songs that have words written about salvation, or testimonial songs about how good God has been to us. These are cheerful and happy songs. "Amazing Grace" is a great example, as is "Brighten the Corner Where You Are." Of course, the church songbook has hundreds of good songs to use. Spiritual songs are usually "religious" songs, meaning their words talk about God, Jesus, the Bible, etc., but spiritual songs can also be good, wholesome songs that are bright and cheerful and put a smile on one's face and a lighter step to his feet. Just be sure the words are spiritually and religiously correct.

God is working on our own spirit here. He knows His Spirit is effective only to the degree that our human spirit is positive and open. The words of the psalms, hymns, and spiritual songs help cheer our spirits and open our spirits to be filled with God's Holy Spirit. Please note how important the **words** of a song are to a Christian. Before God wants us singing the songs, He wants us "speaking" the songs. Don't simply choose songs that make your toes tap; choose songs that educate your heart and teach your mind and spirit the truth of God through the words. There is some great doctrine in many of those hymns and gospel songs in our church hymnals.

2. **Singing and making melody in your heart to the Lord.** Next, notice that God commands us in Ephesians 5:19 to be, "*...singing and making melody in your heart to the Lord.*" Certainly, we know what singing means. Every Christian ought to be a "singer." I don't mean a public per-

former or even a member of the church choir; I'm referring to singing *"unto the LORD."* God gave you a voice; use it for Him. He doesn't care about your tone or pitch or musical talents or your lack thereof. He wants you to sing to Him and for Him just as the birds who sing in the woods when nobody but God hears.

Making melody literally means to play an instrument. Recently, we launched a massive music program in our Hammond Baptist School System. Every student from fourth through eighth grade is required to learn to play a musical instrument and to sing. For other grades, it is optional. When I was in fourth grade, I began playing the saxophone. Hundreds of times I have poured out my heart in pain and in joy through that saxophone. Music is such a powerful medicine for the soul and spirit of man; unfortunately, most Christians never learn to sing or play anything other than the radio or the CD player. God is commanding us to do the singing and the playing, not to listen to someone else do it for us. I firmly believe that our overemphasis on listening to music—good or bad—rather than singing and playing instruments ourselves unto the Lord, is a major contributor to the lack of spiritual influence in our world today.

It's early in the morning; I just got up; and I want to be filled with the Spirit of God. How do I accomplish this goal? The first thing I must do is to surround myself with the right kind of music, but more than that, I'm going to start by reading the words to the Psalms. Then I will begin speaking and singing the right kind of music.

To God be the glory, great things He hath done.
So loved He the world....

"I've got the joy, joy, joy, joy / Down in my heart, (Where?)

[65]

Down in my heart, (Where?)
Down in my heart. / I've got the joy, joy, joy, joy
Down in my heart, / Down in my heart to stay."

God says to speak to ourselves in psalms and hymns and spiritual songs. When I do that, I begin to find my heart tender and my spirit lifted.

Now, I'm not suggesting singing at the top of your lungs in your living room, driving your family crazy. I'm talking about going outside, perhaps into the woods, and singing the great songs of the faith like, *Amazing grace, how sweet the sound that saved a wretch like me....* Sing to yourself.

One characteristic of Brother Hyles was that he was always singing. Every time I was with him, he was singing. When he wasn't talking or counseling, he was always singing; perhaps a little off-key, but he loved to sing or hum or whistle. In many of his sermons, he would sing or whistle. Sometimes he would call and want me to go with him on a driving trip. He'd say, "Our wives are out preaching an evangelistic campaign somewhere. Why don't we go for a drive and get a bite to eat?" As I drove him, if I wasn't asking him questions or if he wasn't talking to me, he would always hum a song, whistle a song, or sing a song. In fact, I cannot recall when he didn't hum or sing or whistle. When we went to the airport together, he'd whistle away. He would get on the airplane whistling; and nine times out of ten somebody would say, "You sound like a happy man." He would always answer, "I am a happy man." He was also a Spirit-filled man.

How was Brother Hyles filled with the Spirit? He sang. How do you get filled with the Spirit of God? What did you hum this morning? Did you hum something from Led Zeppelin, DC Talk, The Beatles, or from some rapper? I don't care if you call it Christian rap, Christian rock, or

Christian contemporary music, that so-called Christian music is like saying, "We're having a Christian fornication party," or "I'm going to commit Christian adultery," or "I'm going to smoke a Christian cigarette or drink a Christian beer." What foolishness!

What kind of music is psalms, hymns, and spiritual songs? Take the Psalms; there are 150 of them. *"I will sing of the mercies of the Lord forever. I will sing. I will sing." "Search me, O God, and know my heart today...."* Sing the Psalms; make up your own tunes! God doesn't care what it sounds like; He says, *"Speaking to yourselves in psalms and hymns and spiritual songs, singing and making melody in your heart to the LORD."*

How do you become filled with the Holy Spirit? Ephesians 5:19 says, *"Speaking to yourselves in psalms and hymns and spiritual songs...."* If your excuse is that you can't sing, speak to yourself a psalm. Read Psalm 1:1a out loud, *"Blessed is the man that walketh not in the counsel of the ungodly."* That's speaking a psalm. Take your songbook, like I have done thousands of times, and read the songs.

I believe the second most important book in your life is the songbook. Everybody should own a songbook, and everyone should go through it every day for a few minutes. Sometimes I have spent hours going through scores of songs—singing some and quoting some. Good ideas will come from those songs.

> *"Be not dismayed what e'er betide. / God will take care of you; Beneath His wings of love abide. / God will take care of you./ God will take care of you, / Thru' ev'ry day, / O'er all the way. He will take care of you, / God will take care of you.*

Say the words! In doing so, you speak to yourselves in psalms, hymns, and spiritual songs.

3. "Giving thanks always." How do you get filled

with the Holy Spirit! Ephesians 5:20 says, *"Giving thanks always for all things unto God and the Father in the name of our Lord Jesus Christ."* What does that verse mean? Tell God, "Thank You." "Thank You, God, for saving my soul." If you will ask God what to thank Him for, He'll tell you.

Every morning while on my knees, I say, "God, tell me some things for which You want me to be thankful. What kind of thankfulness would You like to hear this morning? What menu?" I like to think of myself every morning as a waiter; and as a waiter, I think of myself as giving God a menu and saying, "God, You choose from that menu what you want me to serve You, and I'll serve it."

God says, "Okay, thank Me for your wife."

I reply, "Wow! I have no problem with that. Thank You. I've got the best wife in the entire world."

God says, "That's right. *'...a prudent wife is from the LORD.'* (Proverbs 19:14) *'Whoso findeth a wife findeth a good thing, and obtaineth favour of the LORD.'* " (Proverbs 18:22)

I start thanking God for my wife. Then maybe He'll bring to my mind to ask me to thank Him for my parents or my staff or my team who works with me or the faculty or the students. I'll thank God for things in my life, and as I find myself thanking Him, I find my spirit soaring.

Not only should I be thanking God, I must be expressing my gratitude to others as well. Certainly, my gratitude must begin with God, but my gratitude should extend to others as well. Gratitude is a spirit-filled attitude. I do not know of a more powerful evidence of a spirit-filled person than the evidence of gratitude. We live in a crude generation. We are fast losing our spirit of kindness and gratefulness.

4. "Submitting yourselves one to another." How does one get filled with the Holy Spirit? Verse 21 says, *"Submitting yourselves one to another in the fear of God."* How can I do that? Perhaps your wife says, "Listen, I'm so busy today, and I need to launder a load of whites. Is there any way you could help me?"

"I can do that. In fact, I'll take care of the rest of the laundry for you."

"You would?"

"Yes, I'd be glad to." True, you might shock her into a stroke, but tell me what is wrong with a loving husband helping out a busy wife on a hectic day with the so-called house chores. I want to so live my life so that every day I am looking for ways to fulfill the request of another. Why? We get filled with the Spirit of God by submitting ourselves one to another. I'm not saying to serve only someone in authority, although that's one way of fulfilling this verse. I'm talking about "submitting ourselves one to another."

Let me address those who think that I hold the highest position at First Baptist Church of Hammond. If I am to submit myself, how can I submit myself to somebody higher than I? In your thinking, everybody is lower than I am. How then do I submit to somebody who is higher than I? I cannot. I learned to submit to my roommates while I was in college. I also learned to submit myself to bus kids and to people who couldn't do anything for me. The more you submit to those who cannot promote you or who can't do anything for you or who can't make you look good in another's eyes or who can't mention your name from the pulpit or who can't give you a promotion or a higher position, the more you are allowing God to fill you with His Spirit. That's exactly what God says He wants you to do. Submit yourselves one to another.

A wife will never submit to her husband until she learns to submit to someone who's not a higher authority than she is. If a wife is willing to submit to a peer at school, I guarantee you she will submit to a husband who is a God-given authority over her. If you'll learn to submit to your co-work-ers on your church bus route, I guarantee you'll submit to your employer. You learn to submit to authority by submit-ting to people who are not your authority.

How do you get filled with the Holy Spirit of God? Every day you get up, say, "I'm going to read and sing a Psalm." Quote one such as Psalm 1, *"Blessed is the man that walketh not in the counsel of the ungodly, nor standeth in the way of sinners, nor sitteth in the seat of the scornful. But his delight is in the law of the LORD; and in his law doth he meditate day and night. And he shall be like a tree planted by the rivers of water, that bringeth forth his fruit in his season; his leaf also shall not wither; and whatsoever he doeth shall prosper."* (Psalm 1:1-3) That one was so good, God, I'd like to read another one! You read Psalm 19:7: *"The law of the LORD is perfect converting the soul...."* (Psalm 19:7) You say, "I've got to find another one," so you continue reading or quoting the Psalms.

What happens when you sing songs, when you speak hymns, when you give thanks to God, and when you sub-mit yourselves to one another? II Kings 2:9 is one of the key verses for understanding how to be filled with the Spirit of God. *"And it came to pass, when they* [that's Elijah and Elisha] *were gone over* [Jordan], *that Elijah said unto Elisha, Ask what I shall do for thee, before I be taken away from thee. And Elisha said, I pray thee, let a double portion of thy spirit be upon me."* Notice that Elisha didn't ask for a double portion of God's spirit to be upon him. He said, "Let a double portion of *thy* spirit be upon me."

In the Bible, Elijah performed a total of six recorded mir-acles. Twelve miracles are recorded for Elisha. Every Bible student knows that seemingly Elisha was used on twice as many occasions as Elijah was used. Was he used by God in a spiritual way? My obvious deduction is that he must have been filled with the Spirit of God—perhaps even more than

Elijah was. Why? The reason was that he learned the secret from watching Elijah; and that secret is, if I can open my spirit, that will allow Your Spirit, God, to work through me.

How do you get filled with the Spirit of God? Quite simply, open up your spirit. You get filled with God's Spirit by making it possible for the Spirit of God to work through you.

Ephesians 4:30a says, *"And grieve not the holy Spirit of God."* If I can be filled with the Holy Spirit of God, then I can also grieve the Holy Spirit of God. Verses 31 and 32 tell how a person can grieve the Holy Spirit, *"Let all bitterness, and wrath, and anger, and clamour, and evil speaking, be put away from you, with all malice: And be ye kind one to another, tender-hearted, forgiving one another, even as God for Christ's sake hath forgiven you."* The kind of statement a person with a closed spirit makes is, "Oh, I can't stand that person. Every time I get around him I see red." You are closing your spirit, and God's Spirit can't work through you.

I do not personally believe it is your responsibility to "get the Spirit." You don't get the Spirit, and you don't fill yourself with the Holy Spirit of God. A person doesn't get the Spirit and shove Him into your life. You allow the Holy Spirit to fill your life. Every Christian should know that there's something wonderful called the fullness of the Holy Spirit. How do I get the fullness of the Holy Spirit? By not trying to work on the Spirit of God but by trying to work on me. Nothing is wrong with the Spirit of God; He's not broken. It isn't like asking, "Holy Spirit, what's the matter with You? Why don't You work through me?"

God says, "Your attitude is why! I can't work through a person who's bitter, unforgiving, full of malice, or unkind." All of those words are spirit words. What are spirit words? When you insultingly say, "What's the matter with him today?" Those are spirit words. When you snap back at someone, "Shut up. Leave me alone. I'm having a bad day," those words reveal your spirit. All those are spirit words.

Saying, "I won't forgive her until Hell freezes over," and then praying, "Holy Spirit, please fill me," won't work. The problem isn't God; the problem is me. If a person's spirit is all bottled up or shut off, he cannot get the message. Anger, malice, and unkindness shut off the Spirit. An unforgiving heart shuts off the Spirit, and God says, "I can't get in. Let Me in." However, if you'll open your spirit wide, God says, "I can really fill it."

Isaiah 58:1 says, *"Cry aloud, spare not, lift up thy voice like a trumpet...."* People will say, "What's the matter with Him?" When your spirit's closed up and you're trying to preach the Gospel, you'll say, "Nothing's happening. The altar's not full. What's the matter with me?" You! You! You're the problem! God says, "Get rid of your malice, unkindness, unforgiveness, wrath, and anger; instead, open up your spirit. Speak to yourselves in psalms." When I quote, *"The heavens declare the glory of God; and the firmament sheweth his handywork,"* I am opening my spirit.

> *I will sing of the mercies of the Lord forever;*
> *I will sing! I will sing!*
>
> *I've got the joy, joy, joy...."*

You say, "You're an idiot." Yes, but I'm one happy idiot—one spirit-filled idiot. I noticed Sunday night the altar was pretty full. We had 1,087 sinners walk the aisle on one Sunday and get saved, and 385 of them got baptized. Why? Because a whole lot of people around here are not closing themselves off from the Spirit. These people say, "I'm happy. I've got a right spirit. I'm not angry. I don't have wrath or malice. You can't hurt me because I want the power of Almighty God. I will forgive you."

If you have a grumpy spirit, it's mighty difficult to go soul winning, pass out tracts, knock on doors, and tell people how to get saved.

When you get up in the morning, speak to yourself in psalms and hymns and spiritual songs, and say, "God, I'm so happy!" Give thanks in all things. Say, "My bills aren't all paid, but I've got a job. Thank You for that. Somebody wants to pay me to work; thank You, God!" Take off the restrictions that work at holding back the Holy Spirit.

Yes, certainly there's more to it, but anyone can begin working on this. Open your Bible to the book of Psalms, and start reading in the morning. Start quoting verses at the beginning of the day. Open your songbook; start reading, and saying them, and then start singing. Keep the songs, hymns, and spiritual songs in your life. Then, look for and find ways to submit to people who cannot promote you at all. Find ways to do a good deed for somebody else. Say, "Can I do that for you, please? May I help you with that, please? May I do that for you? I'll be glad to do that. May I volunteer?"

God says, "That person's spirit is opening, and when that spirit is open, My Spirit can work through him." This is what the Word of God tells us to do, step by step, to be filled with the Holy Spirit. This is the recipe! Now, obey it!

CHAPTER FOUR

Evidence of Being Filled with the Holy Spirit

■   ■   ■

I am amazed that so many mature Christians do not know what it means to be filled with the Holy Spirit. There are so many theological ideas and so much spookiness about the subject that people seem to walk right past and miss what it means to be filled with the Spirit. I do not believe being filled with the Holy Spirit is that complicated.

This chapter will be a very practical study of several Scriptures and of some simple observations not of a theological treatise on pneumatology (the doctrine of the Holy Spirit). Rather it will be a very simple and practical teaching that will affect each Christian right down where he lives on a daily basis. Dr. Jack Hyles, my father-in-law and former pastor, loved to quote one of his heroes, Dr. Bob Jones, Sr., about making truth simple. Dr. Bob would say, "Put the jelly down on the bottom shelf where everyone can reach it." That philosophy is for this chapter. Let's look at several examples of those about whom it has been said were filled with the Holy Spirit.

What Does It Mean to Be Filled with the Holy Spirit?

Luke 1:39-45 says, *"And Mary arose in those days, and went into the hill country with haste, into a city of Juda; And entered into the house of Zacharias, and saluted Elisabeth. And it came to pass, that, when Elisabeth heard the salutation of Mary, the babe leaped in her womb; and **Elisabeth was filled with the Holy Ghost:** And she spake out with a loud voice, and said, Blessed art thou among women, and blessed is the fruit of thy womb. And whence is this to me, that the mother of my Lord should come to me? For, lo, as soon as the voice of thy salutation sounded in mine ears, the babe leaped in my womb for joy. And blessed is she that believed: for there shall be a performance of those things which were told her from the Lord."*

Mary, the mother of Jesus Christ, was visiting her cousin Elisabeth. As soon as Elisabeth was filled with the Holy Ghost, she blessed her cousin. The word *blessed* means "to speak well of, to praise somebody, to commend or compliment somebody, or to thank somebody." *Blessing* means "being thankful, speaking well of, being kind, or praising a loved one." Notice that Elisabeth was praising a family member. I have been asked, "How do I know if I'm filled with the Holy Spirit?" If I read these Bible verses correctly and if I understand this passage, I have to ask, "What's your attitude toward your family?" Perhaps your family has disappointed you or broken your heart. Is your attitude right? Mary was expecting a child, but she was not officially married. She was legally bound to Joseph, but the baby she was carrying was not his. This situation could have been a very scandalous affair. Even Joseph had to have the incident explained to him by an angel from God. Her spirit-filled cousin Elisabeth receives her and with discernment accepts her and blesses her.

Luke 1:39-45 contains one of the few conversations recorded of Mary and Elisabeth speaking together. Mary had gone to her cousin's house. As soon as Elisabeth heard the good news about the coming birth of Jesus Christ, she was filled with the Spirit of God. The first thing she did after being filled was to brag on Mary. *"And blessed is she that believed: for there shall be a performance of those things which were told her from the Lord."* (Luke 1:45)

Elisabeth was saying, "I believe God has something special for you in your future."

Do you talk to family members like Elisabeth talked to Mary? How do you talk to your kid-brother or your kid-sister? How do you talk to your family members? Do you speak in a derogatory manner, look down on them, or speak evil of them? Are you jealous or skeptical or suspicious? How do you know you're filled with the Holy Spirit? I read that a good, old-fashioned Bible lady from the hill country received a visit from a cousin. She said, "I heard some good news. I heard my cousin is expecting a baby, and I'm happy for her."

When you hear good news about a family member, how do you react? How do you feel about your sisters and brothers in Christ receiving good news? Suppose a friend or fellow worker is promoted; how do you respond to that situation?

Another statement I hear is, "Brother Schaap, I don't know how to be filled with the Holy Spirit," or "I must not be filled with the Holy Spirit because I don't see the miracles that Jesus did in the Bible happening in my life." The Bible records that Jesus and His disciples laid their hands on people, causing those people to see or to be healed of all their diseases. That kind of power was wonderful, and certainly it does happen in this day and age, but the Bible says Jesus healed people to prove that He was the Son of God.

John 20:30 and 31 says, *"And many other signs truly did Jesus in the presence of his disciples, which are not written in this book: But these are written, that ye might believe that Jesus is the Christ, the Son of God; and that believing ye might have life through his name."* The signs were not to show what it means to be filled with the Spirit.

Having Holy Spirit power doesn't necessarily mean that your bus route will grow suddenly or dramatically. It doesn't necessarily mean that instantly you will be promoted to a higher position. Being filled with the Holy Spirit means that when people you know well have good things happen to them, you are full of praise and compliments because you are happy for them.

What Does It Mean to Be Filled with the Holy Spirit?

When I hear statements like, "My friend just heard he received a promotion; I'm so happy for him." I would put my vote on that person's being filled with the Holy Spirit. "I just got news from home! My sister made cheerleader at our Christian school. Boy, I'm happy for her!" Delight and joy in a sister's success is a good sign you're filled with the Holy Spirit. "I just heard my younger brother beat my soccer record. God bless him! I'm so proud of him!" That rejoicing is a good sign you might be filled with the Holy Spirit. "I just learned that my best friend had a date with a young man she's wanted to date. I've been praying for her! I'm so happy for her!" I would tend to believe that joyful friend is filled with the Holy Spirit.

Were Mary and Elisabeth happy for each other? Yes! Perhaps that is why Mary was chosen to have the baby Jesus and why Elisabeth was chosen to give birth to John the Baptist. These two babies became the two greatest men who

[78]

ever lived, Jesus Christ and John the Baptist. Some relatives might have greeted Mary with hateful words like, "Oh, so who do you think you are, blessed Mary? You think you're going to have the Son of God?" Having a snide, sneering, cynical, critical, caustic attitude is definitely not being filled with the Holy Spirit. The honest, simple truth is that it is easier to weep with those who weep and grieve with those who grieve than it is to rejoice with those who rejoice. One of the big tests of being filled with the Holy Spirit is not how sad you are when someone you know suffers loss, but rather how sincerely delighted you are when that person receives honor and recognition and promotion.

Luke 2:25-35 says, *"And, behold, there was a man in Jerusalem, whose name was Simeon; and the same man was just and devout, waiting for the consolation of Israel:* **and the Holy Ghost was upon him.** *And it was revealed unto him by the Holy Ghost, that he should not see death, before he had seen the Lord's Christ. And he came by the Spirit into the temple: and when the parents brought in the child Jesus, to do for him after the custom of the law, Then took he him up in his arms, and blessed God, and said, Lord, now lettest thou thy servant depart in peace, according to thy word: For mine eyes have seen thy salvation, Which thou hast prepared before the face of all people; A light to lighten the Gentiles, and the glory of thy people Israel. And Joseph and his mother marvelled at those things which were spoken of him. And Simeon blessed them, and said unto Mary his mother, Behold, this child is set for the fall and rising again of many in Israel; and for a sign which shall be spoken against; (Yea, a sword shall pierce through thy own soul also,) that the thoughts of many hearts may be revealed."*

This passage says Simeon was filled with the Spirit of God. He went to church, and he was good to the people he saw. Those two characteristics were the outward manifestations of Simeon's being filled with the Holy Spirit. When

Simeon went to the temple and saw a couple with a little baby, he went out of his way to say, "I want to tell you how happy I am for you."

Being filled with the Holy Spirit is not getting in a shoving match with an usher. I actually had an usher report that he separated a young man from a church usher. The usher was being kind, but he got pushed and shoved and even sworn at. I did not want to know the name of that young man because I did not want to find out it was someone I knew. One thing I know for sure, that young man was **not** filled with the Holy Spirit.

Simeon blessed Joseph and Mary as they entered the temple with Jesus. What does that mean? He praised them. He complimented them. He was thankful for them. He was honored to meet them.

What Does It Mean to Be Filled with the Holy Spirit?

How do you treat your fellow church members? Do you walk into church and say, "I'm glad I have these people sitting near me." If you see someone needing a seat, do you say, "May I give you my seat? I came early, and I got a good seat, but I want you to have it." Being filled with the Holy Spirit is when the usher asks, "Can we have someone sit in the middle?" and you say, "Let me move down; I'll give you the end seat."

You ask, "That's being filled with the Spirit of God?"

How do you read and interpret that passage about Simeon? He surely didn't speak in tongues. The reference doesn't say he won a soul there. Certainly I believe winning people to Christ is part of being filled with the Holy Spirit. Luke 2 says Simeon walked into the temple, the Holy Ghost came upon him, and he walked up to a couple and said,

"May I compliment you for coming here? God bless you. I'm so proud of you for bringing your son to the temple." Certainly his words were prophetic in their theological importance, but practically speaking, he was used to be a great encouragement to Joseph and Mary, this young married couple with a brand new baby boy.

What is your attitude about the people with whom you attend church? Do you sit in judgment and make comments like, "Hypocrite. Every time she sings, my skin crawls because I think she's a fake." In Bible times, someone might have said, "Joseph, who are you to rear the Son of God? Joseph, who do you think you are anyway? You're not even the natural father of that child. What makes you think you're qualified to be that child's daddy?"

A good synonym for *spirit* is the word "attitude." Being filled with the Spirit is being filled with the attitude of God. If a comment is made about a certain person like, "He has such a good spirit," does that statement mean he's walking around speaking in tongues? Too many have the mentality that being filled with the Spirit of God is walking around with a sanctimonious face and carrying a giant print family Bible for a New Testament soul-winner's Bible. That's not what being filled with the Spirit is. The word *attitude* is not found one time in the Bible, but the word *spirit* is found again and again and again.

What Does It Mean to Be Filled with the Holy Spirit?

Luke 4:1 and 2a say, *"And Jesus being full of the Holy Ghost returned from Jordan, and was led by the Spirit into the wilderness, Being forty days tempted of the devil...."* Luke 4:13 and 14 continue, *"And when the devil had ended all the temptation, he departed from him for a season. And Jesus returned in the power of the Spirit into Galilee: and there went out a fame of him through all the region round about."*

Being filled with the Spirit means saying "No" to temptation. Suppose your friends turn on rock music in the car in which you are riding. Do you say, "I don't think we ought to listen to that music"? Or do you say nothing because you are thinking, "If I do that, it'll offend them."

Being filled with the Holy Spirit means being tempted but doing right in the face of temptation. The Devil came to Jesus for 40 days and tempted Him. Every time Satan had an idea, Jesus had a better idea: "Let's obey God." When the Devil realized that he had failed, he left. The Bible said Jesus was filled with the Holy Ghost.

What Does It Mean to Be Filled with the Holy Spirit?

Does it mean speaking in tongues? Entire religions or religious movements are built on one little attribute of the Holy Ghost—speaking in tongues. No tongues are mentioned in these three accounts.

Some religions hold healing services. There is no mention of anyone's being healed when he was filled with the Holy Spirit. Neither Simeon nor Elisabeth nor Mary nor Jesus healed anyone in these Scriptures; however, all of them were filled with the Holy Ghost. How is your attitude toward fellow church members? How is your attitude toward your family?

What Does It Mean to Be Filled with the Holy Spirit?

Do you say "No" to your friends when they tempt you to do wrong? When your friends get off work early and want to visit a nightclub, do you go? A young person filled with the Holy Spirit says, "No, I have a better idea. Let's do right."

The Bible doesn't say Jesus preached a sermon to the Devil. The Bible doesn't say Jesus said, "I can't believe you're doing that!" Jesus didn't launch a tirade; He simply said, "I have a better idea: let's obey God."

"Jesus, were You filled with the Holy Spirit?"

"Yes, I was," He said.

"How did You know You were?"

"When the Devil came and tempted Me, I said, 'I've got a better idea: I'll obey God.'"

"Did You heal anybody?"

"Later I did. Later when God gave Me an earthly ministry, I had to prove that I was the Son of God. I did some healing because the Bible said in the Old Testament that as the Son of God I would heal people."

"Did You speak in tongues?"

"No, I knew Hebrew and Greek, but that's about the only tongues. When I was hanging on the cross, I spoke in Aramaic."

"You didn't do anything wild or crazy?"

"Well, I walked on water, but so did my top disciple Peter, who later abandoned me. The Bible doesn't say anything about his being filled with the Spirit of God when we walked on the water. We were in trouble, and he needed a little confidence. That particular reference is talking about faith."

"Did You have any big miracles, Jesus?"

"Yes, I had several big miracles, but most of those miracles were to emphasize Who I Am and to build confidence in my followers and to increase their faith. Most of the miracles I performed I chose to do privately, simply because I loved the individuals and wanted to help them."

Those miracles were not the evidences of Holy Spirit fullness. No, being filled with the Holy Spirit is going to church, being happy about people who come, treating them nicely, decently, and politely. Bless them as you walk up and down the rows, saying, "Good morning. I'm glad you're here. God bless you."

To be very honest, I know that I am filled with the Holy Spirit of God. One reason why I get to church early is to visit with people. I walk up and down the rows of pews in the auditorium to greet people. That is what it means to be filled with the Holy Spirit. Walking up and down, shaking everybody's hand, and saying, "I'm so glad you're here. God bless you. Can I help you?"

A lady stopped me and said, "I've got a bone to pick with you."

I answered, "What can I do?"

She replied, "These chairs are in my way!"

"Let me get them out of the way for you," I said, as I pulled them out of the way.

What was I doing? I was showing how to be filled with the Spirit of God.

It's no more arrogant to say, "I'm filled with the Spirit of God," than it is to say, "I'm saved." God saved me, and God also fills me with the Holy Spirit; I have to show the manifestation. The manifestation of being saved is acting like a Christian. Am I proud or arrogant because I say, "Thank God I'm saved, and I'm going to live right and live for God?" No! The Bible commands me to live right. The Bible also commands me to be filled with the Holy Spirit.

If you go soul winning on Saturday in obedience to the command and come to church on Sunday and say, "I went out knocking on doors yesterday," you are not bragging; you are obeying a Bible command. God commands the Christian to be filled with the Holy Spirit. Being kind to

[84]

people is one part of being filled with the Holy Spirit of God. Being kind is blessing others. Writing a letter to a loved one and saying, "I just want to tell you I believe in you, and I'm pulling for you," is a part of being filled with the Holy Spirit.

If having the Holy Spirit's fullness is walking around with a halo and being perfect, none of us are qualified. The Bible says in Joel 2:28 and 29, *"And it shall come to pass afterward, that **I will pour out my spirit upon all flesh;** and your sons and your daughters shall prophesy, your old men shall dream dreams, your young men shall see visions: And also upon the servants and upon the handmaids **in those days will I pour out my spirit.**"* The Holy Spirit is for everybody!

What Does It Mean to Be Filled with the Holy Spirit?

How do you act on Wednesday nights when you're at church? Do you sit grumpily in your pew, and when somebody asks, "Are these seats available?" you say, "Find someplace else!" If you do, you're not filled with the Spirit of God!

If you are a college student and if your mother calls you on the telephone and says, "How are you doing today?" and you say, "I'm not feeling very well. I want to come home." You are not filled with the Holy Spirit. You're not blessing your parents.

Suppose you're tempted by your friends or your carpooling crowd, and you agree to go to a party or drink or smoke or look at dirty literature or listen to rock music; you justify your actions and say, "Well, that's not so bad."

Yes, it is bad! Why? You're not filled with the Holy Spirit when you are breaking the commands of God.

What Does It Mean to Be Filled with the Holy Spirit?

Luke 4:18 says, *"The Spirit of the Lord is upon me, because he hath anointed me to preach the gospel to the poor."* Get on a church bus route and tell some people how to be saved. Work in a baptistery or in a dressing room, and help those who walk the aisle prepare to be baptized. Suppose you're hot, tired, perspiring, and hungry, but you still take the time to say to another, "I want to tell you about the greatest news in all the world. I'm going to tell you about Jesus Christ." That is being filled with the Holy Spirit. Preaching the Gospel to others is being filled with the Holy Spirit.

While I was working on a Chicago bus route, I remember meeting a large lady who had a tiny baby. She decided to ride the bus to church. Her little baby kept burping up "white yogurt" all over her shoulder. It was about 90 degrees on the bus, and she was sitting right by me. The smell was so bad that I kept getting the dry heaves. Truthfully, I did not feel very Holy Spirit-filled. That day happened to be the biggest day in the history of my bus route. I preached the Gospel and many were saved. I didn't finish the day feeling like I was filled with the Spirit of God, but I saw a whole lot of poor people accept Christ as their Saviour that day. When poor people get the Gospel preached to them, somebody is filled with the Holy Spirit.

Isn't it interesting that some look for tongues, some look for an ecstatic feeling, or some look for a substitute for some feeling the world provides? Nothing in the Bible says anything about how a person feels when he is filled with the Holy Spirit of God. The Bible does speak about how a person should behave when he is filled with the Holy Spirit of God. The Bible does speak about a person's attitude toward his family, his attitude toward those with whom he goes to church, his attitude toward his loved ones, and his attitude toward those he calls brothers, sisters, cousins, relatives, mom, dad, grandpas, and grandmas. The Bible does speak about getting along with people.

The key chapter and verse in the Bible about being filled with the Holy Spirit is Ephesians 5:18 which says, *"And be not drunk with wine, wherein is excess; but* **be filled with the Spirit.***"*

The world is looking for a "rush," a feeling from some kind of emotion that makes them feel like they're another person. When a person gets drunk, he becomes a different person. When a person takes recreational drugs like ecstasy or heroin or cocaine, he becomes a different person. God says that being filled with the Spirit of God is not having some "rush." He says being filled with the Holy Sprit is not something a person takes in that makes him feel a certain way; rather, it is something inside that makes him live outwardly in a different way.

What Does It Mean to Be Filled with the Holy Spirit?

Ephesians 5:19 continues, *"Speaking to yourselves in psalms and hymns and spiritual songs, singing and making melody in your heart to the Lord."* To what kind of music are you listening? The Bible says to listen to psalms, hymns, and spiritual songs. I can guarantee that the grumpy people who sit as far back in church as they can, who are rude to the ushers, who are unkind to other church members, and who are unhappy because of having to go to church three times a week usually find every excuse in the book to get out of church. These people are not filled with the Holy Spirit. Neither are they listening to appropriate music. Improper behavior and inappropriate music go hand in hand. An individual will not be filled with the Holy Spirit of God if he is listening to the wrong kind of music.

When you get up in the morning, what is the first kind of music about which you think? What's the first kind of song on your mind? Do you think of a worldly song? Do you turn on the rock 'n roll music to get you through the Christian life? Do you reach for the alcohol to get you through the Christian life? When verse 18 says, *"And be not drunk...,"* it is not talking about unsaved people. The verse is talking to the church at Ephesus. Paul was saying, "Church people of Ephesus, don't be drunk with wine. Don't seek a way to cope with being a Christian. If you are filled with the Holy Spirit of God, you can cope just fine."

What Does It Mean to Be Filled with the Holy Spirit?

Ephesians 5:20 says, *"Giving thanks always for all things."* The word *blessing* also means "to give thanks." Therefore, when I am giving thanks or I'm blessing another or I'm being kind or I'm thanking God or I'm thanking others, I am being filled with the Holy Spirit. Being filled with the Holy Spirit is an attitude of gratitude. It means I am grateful for what is happening to me.

Have you said, "Thank you" to anybody today? Have you said, "Thank you" to one teacher who made a difference in your life? Have you written a note to say, "Thank you, Brother So-and-so or Mrs. So-and-so. I appreciate your hard work and preparation."

When a faithful church member, Brother Dave Sisson, held the door for me recently, I said, "Thanks, Brother Sisson, for holding the door for me."

He said, "I love you, Brother Schaap."

I said, "I love you, too, Brother Dave."

I believe there is a sweet spirit in First Baptist Church of Hammond. If you'd just stand in the hallway and listen, within five minutes you will hear someone say, "Thanks," or "Can I do that for you?" or "I appreciate that," or "Let me carry that for you." When I hear such statements, I think, "No wonder God blesses First Baptist Church. It is composed of a whole group of people filled with the Holy Spirit."

How many thank-you notes have you written to your leaders? Have you thanked a leader for being an example by giving thanks always?

What Does It Mean to Be Filled with the Holy Spirit?

How big is my church bus route? How much Scripture do I know? Are the people asking me to preach? Am I going to become a deacon yet? Are they going to ask me to preach in Pastors' School this year? If any of those statements are the mark of your spirituality, then you are not filled with the Holy Spirit of God.

The mark of being filled with the Holy Spirit of God is, "Have I written a thank-you note recently? Have I told anybody how glad I am they go to church? Have I been kind to anyone other than my girlfriend or my boyfriend or someone very close to me?"

How Do I Become Filled with the Holy Spirit of God?

Being filled with the Spirit of God is so much easier than many think it is. Being filled with the Spirit of God is as easy as getting saved! You should ask for the indwelling of the Holy Spirit every day. Because salvation is a one-time-only experience, you don't ask for salvation daily. Asking to be filled with the Spirit of God is daily and constantly.

Being filled with the Holy Spirit is not looking for an emotion, nor is it like taking a little sip of Jack Daniel's to try to get some false courage. When I yield, then I behave like I'm supposed to behave. If I listen to a person's music, it will tell me immediately whether or not a person is filled with the Holy Spirit of God.

The truth is that this matter of being filled with the Holy Spirit is a whole lot more down to earth and practical than what most people think. I want the theology of being filled with the Spirit of God, but my Christianity is where I live. I am a Christian, and if I'm a Christian filled with the Holy Spirit of God, then the people whom I meet and greet at church will know that I'm filled. My family and my loved ones will know I'm filled with the Spirit of God. The people whom I meet in the normal path of life will know.

A gentleman saw me in a restaurant, came over to me, and said, "Hey, Pastor, good to see you! Do you remember me?"

I said, "I sure do. It seems that every time I see you, we're getting a bite to eat."

He said, "I just want to thank you for the good spirit you have."

"I want to thank you for the good spirit you have," I replied. Being filled with the Holy Spirit is just being kind to people out in public.

A lady driver bumped into the back left quarter panel of my car. We both pulled our cars into an abandoned parking lot. I got out, looked at her vehicle, and looked at mine. I could immediately see that she had done several hundred dollars worth of damage.

She jumped out and said, "I'm so sorry! I'm so sorry!"

I said, "It's all right. That's why this is called an accident. You didn't get up this morning and plan to hit my car."

She agreed, "No, I didn't." As she talked to me she said, "Thank you for being so kind."

"No problem," I said. "I'm an attorney, and I specialize in lawsuits like this."

She said, "Are you really?"

I said teasingly, "Yes!"

"Okay," she sighed, "do you want my name and all that?"

"Yes," I answered, "but I'm not a lawyer."

"Good!" she said.

"It's worse," I said. "I'm a pastor." I handed her a tract with my picture, and I said, "That's me, and this is my address."

She moaned, "That is worse. Oh, brother, I hit the car of the pastor of First Baptist Church."

"Don't worry about it," I assured her. "I'll just tell 165,000 members what a bad driver you are!"

Probably a dozen times or more that lady thanked me for being so good about the accident. I said, "Ma'am, they make cars every day, but relationships are more important. I'm glad we ran into each other."

Was I filled with the Holy Spirit? I didn't speak in tongues, but I thanked her for being gracious when she ran into me. I didn't win her to Christ, but I did give her a tract. I didn't do any of the strange things that people mistake for being filled with the Holy Spirit. I didn't fall unconscious on the ground and begin flopping and flailing.

Being filled with the Holy Spirit is much more practical and down to earth. Certainly, there are times when the rolling thunder of revival and the grandeur of big days and giant conferences and the miraculous events that startle our normal routine provide evidence of great movings of the

Holy Spirit; yet, being filled with the Spirit should be a daily event manifested by the gracious and courteous behavior and attitude of the child of God.

CHAPTER FIVE

The Garment of Praise

■   ■   ■

More than anything in the world, every Christian needs the help, the guidance, the direction, and the fullness of the Holy Spirit. *All is vain unless the Spirit of the Holy One come down.*

In counseling with people, I find some who say, "Brother Schaap, I'm not sure how the Holy Spirit could work through me. My own spirit is so crushed and so heavy. My own life seems in such disarray. My own marriage is so distraught. My own family is so paralyzed. My own finances are in shambles. Brother Schaap, I want God to use me, but I'm so distracted and so paralyzed by my own heavy spirit. How can the Spirit of God work through me?"

Others have written letters such as, "Brother Schaap, I've accepted the fact that it may take me several months, and maybe some years, before I restore that sweet relationship I had with the Holy Spirit. I know I deeply, deeply grieved the Spirit of God. Is there anything I can do to accelerate that process? Can I help the grief process on behalf of the Holy Spirit?"

Yes, I believe the Christian can help the Holy Spirit get over His grief. If you know you have ignored Him or mistreated Him and if you would like to jump-start that relationship, I have the single most powerful medicinal tool to help the Holy Spirit. It is like a medicine for the Holy Spirit, and taking advantage of that tool will make Him once again willing and able to help you.

You say, "I thought God was so eager to help me." Sometimes we Christians have this false idea that God is begging to use us and that it doesn't matter how we live or what we do. Yes, God does very much want to use us, but it does matter how we live.

I've had children of God make statements like, "God doesn't seem to work in my life! I knock on doors, but the doors get slammed in my face! I pass out tracts that eventually become trodden under foot by the fools who don't want to receive them. I don't have that power of God. It seems as though I am paralyzed spiritually. Why don't I have God's power in my life?" Perhaps you have grieved the Holy Spirit.

The Holy Spirit can be grieved, but you can jump-start that broken relationship with the Holy Spirit, if you really want to do that. Brother Hyles taught that the key to the Holy Spirit working in us is our own spirit. We are three parts: body, soul, and spirit. The spirit of man is the vessel through which the Holy Spirit works. When our spirit is wounded, the Spirit of God cannot work through us like we would like Him to work. There are several reasons why our own spirit becomes broken or wounded.

• **Unconfessed Sin.** Some have unconfessed sin that has built up and built up. We have become so familiar with those sins that they have become a part of our lives and we don't even realize we are sinning. Unconfessed sin builds up, and it grieves the Holy Spirit when a Christian will not deal with his sin.

• **Wayward Children.** The Bible very clearly teaches that children who break their parent's hearts are one of the chief reasons for a heavy spirit in a home. I believe that some teenagers are doing more to stop First Baptist Church of Hammond from reaching the next level than any other single contributing factor. When a teenager causes grief to his parents, insults them, brings them shame, disappoints them, and causes mom's tears and dad's frustrations, he is contributing to their spirit's being quenched. That behavior grieves the Holy Spirit more than any other single factor. The Bible very clearly points out several times in the book of Proverbs that a rebellious child or a child who causes shame to his mom and dad breaks down their spirits, thus hindering the work of the Holy Spirit.

• **Self-Pity.** Nothing hurts an individual's own spirit more than self-pity. Stop feeling sorry for yourself!

• **Sins of Others.** In rare cases, some very holy and godly people get depressed over the sins of others. That category includes such people as Ezra, Daniel, Nehemiah, Moses, and Paul. On rare occasions, some people who see the sins of others and the sins of their nation get so broken and depressed by what they see that their spirits are wounded to the point where they become ineffective for God. Elijah found himself in such a case. He became depressed at what he saw with Jezebel and the prophets of Baal that he went into hiding for a lengthy time.

Regardless of the cause, a depressed spirit limits the Holy Spirit. The most powerful potent medicine, as well as the chief scriptural medicine, for a depressed spirit is one word—*praise*. Nothing jump-starts your spirit, which jump-starts the Holy Spirit, quite like praise.

When we grieve the Holy Spirit, we often misinterpret the result. We think we should go to the doctor because we are not feeling very well. We write off a grieved Holy Spirit as either a bad day, or we resort to psychiatrists, drugs, or pills to influence our grieved spirit. We further grieve the

Holy Spirit by seeking alternative helps.

Again and again in the book of Revelation, the sin of taking drugs is mentioned as being a contributor to moral decay and immorality. The Bible word is *sorceries*. Our modern-day word *pharmacy* is derived from the same Greek word from which sorceries and its companion word witchcraft are translated.

If you took your concordance and looked up the word *witchcraft*, you would discover again and again that God said that practicing *witchcraft* and *sorcery* resulted in much perversion and idolatry, and ultimately judgment from God. Every time those words are found, one would think the references refer to witches and devils. However, those devils are usually found in the pills that Christians take by the millions to replace that which only the Holy Spirit can provide.

I'm not talking about aspirin or the prescription medicines you need because a wise doctor or a godly man helped you, but I'm talking about Christians overdosing on pills—some to boost them up, some to bring them down, and some to level them out. It is abuse by the American Medical Association and others to try to make you or give you what only the Spirit of God can give you. There is certainly a place for good doctors and medicine.

Far too many Christians who are having a bad day say, "I think I need to pop in a video to watch." Maybe you do, but the videos you watch will not help the Holy Spirit at all. Some might say, "I think I need to run down to the psychiatrist. Maybe he'll give me a prescription or an injection."

Too many Christians are running to the psychiatrist instead of running to praise. Running to the psychiatrist compounds the problem by further depressing your spirit and by further suppressing the Holy Spirit. A suppressed Holy Spirit brings further shame, reproach, and grief to the Holy Spirit. No depressed person has the energy, response, or results he wants. A heavy spirit often paralyzes us into inactivity, and that inactivity only worsens our moods. What we say is, "Well, those pills aren't making me feel any better. I don't feel like going out today."

We have become paralyzed because of a depressed spirit. Self-pity, unconfessed sin, or grief brings that paralysis to us. Once we get paralyzed, our spirit becomes depressed. In our depressed state we say, "I don't feel like doing anything. I don't feel like going out soul winning or passing out tracts. I don't feel like knocking on doors. I don't feel like healing anybody else's spirit. I'm so depressed myself that I don't want to do anything."

As a result, we pop more pills, and once again that doesn't work. So we watch more television, but talk shows with hosts like Jenny Jones and Jerry Springer do not help. We try the soap operas, and soon we find that the rest of the world is as miserable as we are. Misery loves company! So, we get all wrapped up in another's messed-up life, become paralyzed into inactivity, and then wonder, "Where is that joy in the Christian life? Where is that victorious Christian living?"

Many scriptural ways of restoring our spirit exist; however, the chief scriptural healing medicine for a heavy spirit is praise. Why is praise so powerful? The great prophet said in Isaiah 61:3, *"...to give unto them...the garment of praise for the spirit of heaviness...."* That verse contains the answer. The person who clothes himself in praise will do more to help his heavy spirit than any kind of pills, any psychiatrist or any psychologist—Christian or otherwise—or anything else.

Psalm 149 says, *"Praise ye the LORD. Sing unto the LORD a new song, and his praise in the congregation of saints. Let Israel rejoice in him that made him: let the children of Zion be joyful in their King. Let them praise his name in the dance: let them sing praises unto him with the timbrel and harp. For the LORD taketh pleasure in his people: he will beautify the meek with salvation. Let the saints be joyful in glory: let them sing aloud upon their beds. Let the high praises of God be in their mouth, and a twoedged sword in their hand; To execute vengeance upon the heathen, and punishments upon the people; To bind their kings with chains, and their nobles with fetters of iron. To execute upon them the judgment written this honour have all his saints. Praise ye the LORD."*

To what is this Psalm referring? This Psalm is listing the works of praise.

1. Praise promotes the Word of God. The Bible says, *"Let the high praises of God be in their mouth, and a twoedged sword in their hand."* The twoedged sword is the Word of God. Hebrews 4:12 says, *"For the word of God is quick, and powerful, and sharper than any twoedged sword...."*

God says that even though you have the Word of God in your hand, you cannot use it effectively if you have grieved the Holy Spirit. Have you ever tried to witness to someone, but you felt like your words just bounced off the person? Bus captains or Sunday school teachers, have you ever tried to teach or preach the Bible, but nobody seemed to respond? Even when you say, "Hey, out there, I'm talking to you," nothing happens. The Bible is in your hand, but there is no power from your lips. Why? Because you need praise! Praise empowers the preaching of the Word of God!

You might ask, "Brother Schaap, when you go preach somewhere or before you preach, what do you do? What does a preacher do before he preaches?" I don't know what anybody else does, but I know what I do; I praise God! I get alone in my office, and I spend a long time saying, "God, I want to praise You. I want to talk about You."

Praising God doesn't mean simply saying, "Praise the Lord!" That is restating the commandment, but it's not obeying the commandment. Praise promotes the Word of God.

2. Praise promotes justice. I have heard people make statements like, "I feel like I'm so mistreated. I feel like everybody hates me. Nobody likes me." Too many people who feel that way take some pills or watch television talk shows or go see a psychiatrist to get better. Why not try praising? Praise brings justice into a person's life.

God says, "I would like to right some wrongs in your life. I would like to bring a little leverage into play on some wrongs that have been done in your life." Praise will bring justice.

3. Praise binds the powers of darkness. You say, "I feel so oppressed." Ephesians 6:12 says, *"For we wrestle not against flesh and blood, but against principalities, against powers, against the rulers of the darkness of this world, against spiritual wickedness in high places."* Christian, do you really understand that demonic powers do exist? I'm not a spooky kind of Christian; but I guarantee you this, they are out there.

A highly organized, orchestrated group of demonic warriors are present who are trying to discourage your heart, oppress your spirit, distract your mind, and keep you from doing the will of God. They can and will infect your spirit. Demons do bother Christians. Their work is to weigh down or to press your spirit. They bring negativism as they criticize, scold, rebuke, bring up past sins, and lay guilt trips on you. Then you walk around barely functioning, saying, "Why do I feel the way I do?" There is an unseen spirit with a spiritual two by four hitting you in your spirit.

When you argue with your spouse, do you suddenly realize, "Why am I arguing with you? I don't have a problem with you. Self, shut up; I don't know why I'm saying this." A spiritual weapon is being aimed at you, and those spiritual warriors are shooting at you with fiery darts. They are hitting what they are aiming at, and the darts of doubt, suspicion, guilt, anger, and skepticism are hitting you.

[99]

The question immediately comes, "How can I prevent that from happening? How can I fight that?" The Psalmist said, *"To bind their kings with chains, and their nobles with fetters of iron."* (Psalm 149:8) You don't have to perform any kind of hocus-pocus magic. Simply turn off the television and just start praising God! God will send His strong angels to bind the powers of darkness. Christians, you will not only feel free, but you will have the victory over these evil spirits. These spirits flee when Christians praise God.

Prescription drugs, over-the-counter drugs, and non-recreational drugs will not bind the powers of darkness. Cursing will not bind the powers of darkness. Sending money to all the television evangelists will only make them rich so they can drive a Rolls Royce and live in mansions; but you will still be oppressed. Instead, why don't you start praising God?

4. Praise provides a kind of architecture or a pattern for people to copy. The Bible says in Proverbs 27:21 that a man becomes his praise or his criticism. *"As the fining pot for silver, and the furnace for gold; so is a man to his praise."*

Praise is the balance of judgment. Praise brings a balance in your life. Praise evens out the low spots. Praise brings down the haughty spirit, brings up the oppressed spirit, brings down the proud attitude, and brings up the burdened attitude. Praise brings a leveling power in a person's life.

What does it mean to praise God? What do you do to get God to bind the dark powers? What do you do to empower the Word of God when you stand to teach it to boys and girls, and men and women? What does it mean to praise God? We often say, "Praise God!"

Praising God is a command. Saying, "Praise God!" is like saying, "Read your Bible!" But have you read it? Saying, "Praise the Lord!" is like saying, "Say your prayers!" But have you said your prayers? We often repeat statements and quote commands, but they don't mean anything in our Christian lives.

If you say to your son, "Son, mow the lawn," but if your son runs around the lawn merely repeating your command, "Mow the lawn," the lawn won't be mowed when you get home. You'll then say, "Son, if you don't mow the lawn right now, I'm going to mow you." Repeating a command isn't mowing the lawn.

I can say, "Mrs. Colsten, play that organ." If she repeats my command, "Play the organ," she is not playing the organ.

That is the way many of us look at the Bible. We say, "Well, I tried praising the Lord." I wager you didn't. Most of what the average Christian calls "praising the Lord" is merely repeating the command to praise the Lord, and it's as effective as saying, "Read my Bible," over and over. If I were to ask you what you have read, you'd say, "I read my Bible." You didn't read the Bible; you quoted the command.

From Psalm 149, I want to share four ways every individual can praise the Lord.

*1. **Praise means to sing a hymn.*** Sing a hymn, not that modern, contemporary garbage. A hymn is a song that magnifies the character of God.

> *All hail the pow'r of Jesus' name!*
> *Let angels prostrate fall....*

Quote those stanzas ten times, then tell me how you feel. Quoting words like these from hymns will do ten thousand times more for you than saying, "Praise the Lord! Praise the Lord! Praise the Lord!" If you were to stand in front of a mirror and say, "Praise the Lord," over and over again, you might laugh yourself to health, but you are not praising the Lord. Praising the Lord means to sing a hymn.

Quote the words to a song like:

[101]

"Great is Thy faithfulness," Oh God, my Father,
There is no shadow of turning with Thee;
Thou changest not, Thy compassions, they fail not;
As Thou hast been Thou forever wilt be.

Pardon for sin and a peace that endureth,
Thy own dear presence to cheer and to guide;
Strength for today and bright hope for tomorrow,
Blessings all mine, with ten thousand beside!

Great is thy faithfulness!

Quote the stanzas to that song ten times, and then tell me how depressed you feel. Praise means singing a hymn. Take your songbook, turn anywhere, and start reading.

My sheep know My voice, / And the path that I take.
They follow wherever I go; / My sheep know My voice,
And come at My call, / But a stranger's voice they do not know.

Under His wings I am safely abiding;
Tho' the night deepens and tempests are wild,
Still I can trust Him; I know He will keep me.
He has redeemed, and I am His child.

Under His wings, under His wings,
Who from His love can sever?
Under His wings, my soul shall abide,
Safely abide forever.

I feel good just reading these words!

I am weak but Thou art strong, / Jesus keep me from all wrong;
I'll be satisfied as long,/ As I walk let me walk close to Thee.

Good Gospel songs and hymns like these are what we need. Turn off the radio, quit listening to the contemporary garbage, get a songbook, and read it.

You say, "That's too simple." There is nothing compli-cated about the Christian life. That is why God commands you to praise. He knows you are not a very complicated per-son. He knows you are a simple-minded individual just like I am. It is simple to be saved. It is simple to be sanctified. It is simple to be filled with the Holy Ghost. Too many of us have forgotten the second most important book of our life. The Bible is number one, and the hymnbook is number two.

Hear ye the Master's call. / "Give Me thy best!"
For, be it great or small, / That is His test.
Do then the best you can, / Not for reward,
Not for the praise of man, / But for the Lord."

Just turn anywhere in the hymnbook. Try starting on page one.

All hail the power of Jesus' name!
Let angels prostrate fall....

What a great start! Somebody asked me, "Brother Schaap, when you spend time with God for three hours, how do you do that? I prayed for everything I could think of, and it took me 13 seconds. At four o'clock in the morn-ing? Even Starbuck's coffee can't wake me up at four o'clock in the morning!"

I'll tell you exactly what I do. I go downstairs in my flipflops, in my pajamas, and my bathrobe with my song-book, and I just start reading.

Redeemed—how I love to proclaim it!
Redeemed by the blood of the Lamb;
Redeemed thru' His infinite mercy,
His child, and forever, I am.

[103]

Do that for 30 minutes, then tell me where your depression is. You'll have a hard time finding it. Why? Because praise unlocks the muscle of God. When you start praising, God says, "Come on, Gabriel. Come on, Michael. Saddle up the horses, and let's go be with him!" You will find yourself surrounded and bathed in the love of God.

As we sing our songs at church services, we spend about 15 minutes talking about Him. When the congregation sings, we are boasting about God. Did you notice the overall mood of the auditorium? It just picked up. Why? Because the powers of darkness were being bound. Spirits were being freed from bondage.

2. Praise means to boastfully rave. Ladies, have you ever gotten a new dress and wanted your husband to tell you how you want him to think you look in it? (I had to word that sentence carefully!) When he says, "Wowie, Zowie! You look stunning!" that's an expression of praise.

How do you boastfully rave about God? "I just thought of something, God. You are wonderful! You're awesome! You saved me—a sinner!"

If you say, "That's not my personality," that is why you are depressed, and I'm not. Yes, I was personally trained by Brother Hyles, but so were most of you reading this book! We listened to many of the same sermons. We've been trained by the best, and he taught us to praise God. One of the ways Brother Hyles stayed on top all of the time was by living on a higher plane; he lived on higher ground. He was a man of praise, and that is how he lived, making loud, raving, boastful sounds about God. Brother Hyles never sat around with a grumpy look on his face to prove to everyone how miserable he was.

Child of God, rave about Him! I don't mean to look up at Heaven and say, "Brother Schaap said we're to praise You. Thank You for Your love, Your mercy, the Bible, and all that

[104]

stuff." You won't feel any better. If your wife models a new dress and if you say, "Red's not your color, but it's okay," you'll have to find a couch to sleep on. Why should God get excited when you say, "Oh, nice Book with good words, God. You're a good God." That's not how to praise God. Get excited about God.

What lights your fire? Find what gets you most excited. Of course, I'm speaking of good things, not rock concerts or drugs. What do you get excited about? God says, "I don't care what it is, but make sure you get at least that excited for Me." That's praising God. Be as excited about God as you are for anything else in your life. Rave about Him.

Too often, we cheat God by giving Him second- and third-rate emotions. My Bible says in Romans 1:21, "...*they glorified him not as God....*" What does this verse mean? The people glorified Him, but they gave Him second- or third-rate glory instead of first-rate glory. God is saying, "If I receive second- or third-rate glory, eventually I'll have no glory."

God wants His children to get more excited about Him and what He has done for them than anything else. That excitement is praising God!

Where do you praise God? You praise Him in the car, in your basement, outside your house, anywhere. Lock yourself in a room or go in the bathroom and say to yourself, "I know I'm going to make an idiot of myself," but make an idiot of yourself and start praising God! Try it for 15 minutes.

Don't use the excuse, "It's not my personality." Okay, then what is your personality? What do you get excited about? Is it when your husband says, "I'm going out of town for a couple of days, and here's $200 so you can go shopping."

Do you shout, "I love you! I love you! You're the best

husband in the world!" Do you ever get that excited about God or His Book or His blood or His mercy? God wants His children to boast about Him.

We don't rave about God, but we rave about cars, cosmetics, and clothing. Teenagers rave about a date or a new hairstyle. Do you ever get excited about God like that? When we don't rave about God, we've taken man-made objects, and we've promoted them above God.

3. *Praise means to pacify or soothe with words.* Have you ever comforted God? You say, "Well, He's the God of comfort!" I know, but if you remember, the emotions you have are from Him. Have you ever soothed God? Let me illustrate.

Say, "God, can I chat with You for a few minutes? I want to tell You how I feel. I want to tell You what a great job You did the other day in my church service. I know some people are making fun of You around the country, but I want to tell You that You're A+ in my book, God. The whole world may not understand this, but I believe You and I have got something special. God, there's nobody like You. There's nobody in the world like You! In fact, there are those who are called 'god,' but they're just hunks of wood, steel, or metal. You're a living, breathing God, and You were in the church service this morning. You really knew how to work in people's lives!"

Do you ever talk to God like that? That is how you praise God. When you say, "Praise God!" God says, "Go ahead. Tell Me how good I am. Tell Me how wonderful I am!"

4. *Praise means to confess sin.* God says it's praiseworthy when you agree with Him on how He looks at your sin. We have a wrong attitude about our sin. We're embarrassed by our sin, and we don't want to talk about it, not even with God Who knows all about it because He's God! Every

Christian would have a lot freer spirit if he would just be honest with God and say, "God, I've got to talk to You about something. I'm having a real problem with _____. You know it, and I know it. I'm having a difficult time getting over it, and God, I'm embarrassed about it, but I know You're not. I know You love me, but I've got to talk to You about it, God. I agree with You that it's all wrong, and I'm sorry. God, I'm so weak and so frail, but You're so strong and mighty. The only hope I've got of getting over this is You." Do you ever chat with God like that about your sin?

If you would spend time praising God, you would unleash the mighty power of God, and you would bind the power of darkness. Christians, when you listen to rock 'n roll music or country music, you bind God and release the powers of darkness to oppress your spirit. The wrong kind of music oppresses your spirit.

If you want the Spirit of God to use you, if you feel like you have grieved the Spirit of God, and if you feel like you have somehow wounded His Spirit by wounding your spirit, you can correct this situation. Go home, shut off the television, pick up your songbook, and start singing or reading.

> *I've seen the lightning flashing,*
> *I've heard the thunder roll,*
> *I've felt sins' breakers dashing,*
> *Which almost conquered my soul;*
> *I've heard the voice of my Savior*
> *Bidding me still to fight on;*
> *He promised never to leave me,*
> *Never to leave me alone!*

Lines like that are better than any lines a person like Jay Leno has ever hoped to say in his life. You will find more comfort in lines like that than in any television program you watch. Just praise God! Go ahead, praise God! Get your songbook and rave about Him. When you praise God, you enable the Holy Spirit's power to flow through you.

CHAPTER SIX

Increase My Measure

■ ■ ■

"*He that cometh from above is above all: he that is of the earth is earthly, and speaketh of the earth: he that cometh from heaven is above all. And what he hath seen and heard, that he testifieth; and no man receiveth his testimony. He that hath received his testimony hath set to his seal that God is true. For he whom God hath sent speaketh the words of God: for God giveth not the Spirit by measure unto him. The Father loveth the Son, and hath given all things into his hand. He that believeth on the Son hath everlasting life: and he that believeth not the Son shall not see life; but the wrath of God abideth on him.*" (John 3:31-36)

Whatever so-called secret there is to the Christian life or whatever key there is that unlocks the secret to living the victorious Christian life, that secret cannot be discovered nor will that key be used successfully without the Holy Spirit's direct involvement.

During the years I was at Hyles-Anderson College, both as a student and as an administrator, I often heard a statement made in regard to the chapel preaching. Out-of-town guest speakers or even our own preachers would stand to preach and say, "Listen carefully. I only have 30 minutes, and I have a sermon to give that could change your life. If you will listen, you will hear a life-changing truth."

After hearing that statement many times, a student quipped, "I've heard so many life-changing sermons I don't know who I am anymore!"

We have laughed about that student's humorous comment, but the truth of the matter is, there are many life-changing truths. Every truth has the power to change a portion of a person's life, but whatever life-changing truth he hears is of no effect without the direct aid and involvement of the Holy Spirit.

A person can hear a truth and say, "Wow, that truth is going to change my life." I don't care how powerful a truth is, it won't bring about any lasting change unless the Holy Spirit helps with that truth. A person in and of himself is powerless. As the songwriter penned, *All is vain unless the Spirit of the Holy One comes down.* All is worthless, menial, like sounding brass or tinkling cymbal without the power of the Holy Spirit to help us. In this chapter I want to examine how a person can increase the measure of the Holy Spirit's influence in a his life.

The Bible says in John 3:34, *"For he whom God hath sent speaketh the words of God: for God giveth not the Spirit by measure unto him."* Notice that the word *Spirit* is capitalized, which means it refers to the Holy Spirit. This verse is saying that God did not pour out the Holy Spirit upon Jesus Christ with a measure. The word *measure* is translated from the Greek word *metron* from which we get words such as *meter*. *Measure* refers to an instrument of measurement. John 3:34 teaches us that Jesus was not limited in His fullness of the Holy Spirit during His earthly ministry. As a human man on earth, He was filled by the Spirit. This "filling" was not measured out to Him in any limited measurement. The Holy Spirit was not limited in any way through Jesus Christ.

Unlike the example of Jesus Christ, we often limit God's Spirit. God "measures" out a limited capacity of influence of the Holy Spirit in us.

Psalm 78:41 reads, *"Yea, they turned back and tempted God, and limited the Holy One of Israel."* I don't ever want to limit the Holy One of my life. I want God to increase the measure He uses to determine the degree of influence and power I receive through the Holy Spirit. The Holy Spirit was a constant fountain springing up within Jesus Christ; however, that is not so with all Christians. We do receive the Spirit by measure; however, that measure can be increased.

1. Christ Jesus in His earthly ministry had an unlimited measure of the Spirit. Colossians 1:19 says, *"For it pleased the Father that in him* [Christ] *should all fulness dwell."* Colossians 2:9 says, *"For in him* [Christ] *dwelleth all the fulness of the Godhead bodily."* Everything that God was, all that the Father represented, and all that the Spirit represented were wrapped up in Christ Jesus. No limitations were put on Christ. He did not **need** fresh oil; He **was** fresh oil.

We often sing the chorus,

> *Running over,*
> *Running over,*
> *My cup's full and running over,*
> *Since the Lord saved me,*
> *I'm as happy as can be,*
> *My cup's full and running over.*

Jesus' cup was full and running over because it sprang up within Him. He was filled full constantly with all the fullness of the Godhead, including all the fullness of the Spirit of God.

2. Christians receive the Spirit's influence by measurement. The Spirit is measured to Christians just like a cook preparing a cookie recipe says, "I need a teaspoon of vanilla, a cup of flour, a half cup of pecans, and a half cup of chocolate chips." A cook measures each item, shakes it down, levels it off, and gets just the right amount. God says to a Christian, "Now, I'm going to give you Holy Spirit influence. Since you are saved, I have proportioned the Holy Spirit's influence to you by measure."

I Corinthians 12:7 says, *"But the manifestation of the Spirit is given to every man to profit withal."* This verse is similar to Acts 2: 17b, which says, *"I will pour out of my Spirit upon all flesh."* God is saying, "I will pour out the Holy Spirit on you; I will manifest Him through your life, but I will decide how much you get."

I Corinthians 12:11 says, *"...dividing to every man severally as he will."* God is saying, "I decide how much Spirit control you have or how much 'metron' or 'measure' of the Holy Spirit you receive." As I have already stated, Jesus Christ didn't have any limit on the Holy Spirit fullness in His life; it was unlimited. That omnipotence that Christ had is because of the unlimited flow of the Spirit of God through Him.

Jesus never had to get filled again and again and again with the Spirit. As the source of the Spirit, He was always filled with the Spirit. The Spirit welled up within Him like a well of water. If you want a fountain flowing in you like Christ had flowing in Him, you can have it, but you will have to pay the price for it. Christ, the Son of the Living God, had the Holy Spirit without measure. You may have it by measure if you'd like it.

May I share what I do? I walk to the main auditorium of the First Baptist Church of Hammond nearly every Saturday night, get behind the pulpit, fall on my face before God, and pray. In the same study where Brother Hyles spent 40 years, I fall on my face before God and beg, "Oh, God, if You don't pour out a bigger measure on me, how are we going to help these people? I want that measure increased in my life."

Romans 12:6 says, *"Having then gifts differing…according to the proportion of faith."* God is saying, "I have a proportion for you. I've marked out a boundary on how much you get, but if you'd like to increase your boundaries, you may. If you'd like to lengthen your stakes and strengthen your cords, you may. If you want to tear down your barns and build bigger ones, you may. If you would like a bigger measuring cup, you may have it."

Some people have only a little teaspoon because they haven't asked for any increase in measure. They have accepted that limited measure that God the Father appropriated to them. That little measuring cup has been all that they have been receiving to manifest the Spirit of God.

The pouring out of the Holy Spirit is not an experience. God might choose to give someone an experience, but that's not the point. When you lead someone to Christ, you don't finish talking to your convert by saying, "Have you had the experience?"

I have seen some wonderful, sweet salvation experiences, but the experience is always a by-product. An "experience" is never the Scriptural portion of salvation. Likewise, having an experience is irrelevant to having Holy Spirit fullness. A person does not get saved by experience. He gets saved by placing his faith in Christ, and in His death, burial, and resurrection. How that wonderful salvation affects a person might be due in part to his personality or part of the emotion of the moment or part of the exceeding awareness of the sinfulness of sin or his mental capacity, youthfulness or maturity. A salvation "experience" is often based upon who is with you, your embarrassment, or your nervousness. Likewise, an individual's experience with the Holy Spirit is irrelevant.

[113]

I have had people say to me that they have never had an experience like I have described about my call to preach or about the sweet times God has moved deeply in my spirit. In answer to those comments, I say, "I wasn't trying to have an experience. I was trying to surrender to the Spirit of God, so I said, 'I want a bigger measuring cup. I want more than You allotted or proportioned to me.' I haven't looked for an experience."

I have had some wonderful experiences, but I have never told all of my experiences because I'm so afraid others will say, "That's what I want." I don't care whether or not you have an experience. What I want for you is a bigger cup as God pours out His Spirit of God upon you.

II Kings 2:9 says, "...let a double portion of thy spirit be upon me." When Elisha followed Elijah, he realized that God was using Elijah in a mighty way. Elisha said, "I don't know what you've got Elijah, but I want twice as much." If you study the miracles of Elijah and count carefully, you will find that Elisha performed twice as many miracles as did Elijah.

3. God can be persuaded to use a larger measuring cup when He measures out a portion of the Spirit's power. Is anyone interested in having a larger measure? Is your marriage in trouble? If so, you need the power of God and the Holy Spirit's help. You can read all the books I recommend on marriage, including those written by Brother Hyles, those written by my wife and me, and those written by anyone else with a book on the subject of marriage. You can also get tapes, go to classes, and attend marriage seminars, but *all is vain unless the Spirit of the Holy One comes down.* We must have the Holy Spirit.

Are you having trouble rearing your children? If so, you need the power of the Holy Spirit. Are you having trouble with the will of God? If so, you need the power of the Holy Spirit.

[114]

In the previous chapters, we have learned to be hungry for the power of the Spirit of God, we have learned why we don't have it, and we have learned how to "jump-start" it and get it working again. In this chapter, I want to share ways which allow you to get a bigger measuring cup. There are three specific ways a person can increase the volume of influence the Father allocates to him when he asks for a portion of the Spirit of God.

I.
Yield Yourself
to the Holy Spirit

Many years ago when Brother Hyles taught us to yield to the Holy Spirit seven times a day, I began following his advice. He included several examples of ways to remember to yield to the Spirit. Brother Hyles taught his people to include that time of yielding with scheduled tasks they already were doing. I had a shaving box that held my razor, so I taped a piece of paper on it with the words, "Yield to the Holy Spirit." I haven't needed the reminder of that paper for a long time, and I've gone through many razors since that one, but I began posting the reminders at that time. Then I began to add more times daily that I yielded myself to the Holy Spirit. I worked up to two, three, four, five, six, and seven times a day when I yield myself to the Holy Spirit.

What words a person uses when he asks to be filled with the Spirit may differ from what spirit-filled men like Brother Hyles or Billy Sunday or D.L. Moody or J. Frank Norris or or Dr. Joe Boyd or Dr. Lee Roberson use. The words used are important, but the most important thing is having the time to ask the Holy Spirit for His filling.

I yield to the Holy Spirit in the morning, about midmorning, about noontime, and about mid-afternoon. Before I preach or teach or conduct a meeting or when any kind of a major change occurs in my schedule, I yield myself again. Before I begin counseling people in my office after a service, I shut the door, get on my knees, and yield myself to the Holy Spirit. I yield myself again before I go home. Every time I change gears, I yield myself. Many, many times a day I yield myself.

When I yield, I get on my knees and say, "Heavenly Father, I yield to You the best I know how right now. Father, I ask You to crucify the flesh and to fill me with Your Spirit. I ask You to increase the size of the measure You use to pour out Your Spirit upon me. I pray You would help me to help those You bring across my path as Jesus would if He were in my shoes. Help me to fulfill those works you ordained me to accomplish before the world began."

Basically, praying that simple prayer is all I do. I was taught by the best, and they told me this was how they yielded to the Holy Spirit. So the best I know how, I likewise yield myself to the Holy Spirit.

I know that I cannot know my heart, because my heart is deceitful above all things and desperately wicked, but the best I know how, I yield myself to Him. I asked God to crucify my old flesh that wants to get in the way, that tries to take the credit, and that tries to take the glory that belongs to God. I Corinthians 1:29 says, *"That no flesh should glory in his presence."* Isaiah 42:8 says, *"I am the LORD...and my glory will I not give to another...."*

Many times I say, "Not only do I yield to You, but please crucify my sinful flesh because I cannot crucify myself. Fill me with Your Spirit. Would You increase the measure by which You pour out Your Spirit? I need a bigger measure, God."

I know I need the Spirit of God. You need the Spirit of

God, too, but I don't know if you know you do. Every Christian surely ought to know he needs the Spirit of God. I yield many times a day to the Holy Spirit. My main concern when I yield to Him is knowing what size measuring cup is God using to pour out His Spirit upon me.

Sometimes when I yield, I lay prostrate; sometimes I stand; and I almost always kneel. Sometimes I'm emotional. Sometimes in the middle of praying, the thought occurs to me about just how sweet God is and how good it is that He wants to use a man. Many times I get all choked up. Sometimes it's almost perfunctory. Sometimes I laugh. Sometimes I'm almost in a joking mood—not sacrilegious, of course. I come to God with a little humor. For instance, before preaching out of town I might say, "Lord, if these people **really** knew who I was, they'd never ask me! If I really knew who I was, I wouldn't be asking You!"

God uses man. To me, that thought is almost humorous at times. It is incredible and humbling that God would want to use sinful, mortal man to preach His unsearchable riches. WOW! What a God! WOW! What a privilege to think that God would trust me to stand in His stead and to represent Him! What a privilege to think that God would even consider using me as a vessel of influence through His Holy Spirit!

I have all of those emotions, but being filled with the Holy Spirit is not an emotion nor an experience I am seeking. Yielding is a sincere act on my part. I want that measuring cup by which He pours out that Spirit to be larger.

To be sure, not everyone needs the same size measuring cup. More than likely, not many need as much as Brother Hyles needed. Many years ago, I was sitting in the First Baptist Church auditorium listening to Brother Hyles preaching about the power of God. He used a wonderful illustration and made a statement that made a lot of sense to me as a young preacher boy. His words helped me at that time.

He said, "You young preacher boys come to college and want the same power that Dr. Jack Hyles has, but at this point, you don't need as much as Dr. Jack Hyles has."

I now make that same statement to the young preacher boys at Hyles-Anderson College who say, "I want the power of God." Most of them probably will not pastor a church the size of First Baptist Church of Hammond. As of right now, most of those preacher boys are not pastoring anyone. Some aren't even a bus captain or Sunday school teacher, so they don't need that much. Too many young preacher boys get sidetracked by trying to be like someone else when God says, "That will come in time." Let me share the illustration that Brother Hyles taught.

As a 16 or 17 year old, a young man may get a job delivering newspapers in his neighborhood. Maybe he has 50 papers he has to deliver. He doesn't have a lot of time, so his parents help him find a little cheap car like a Honda Civic that gets good gas mileage. Because Civics get 40 or 50 miles to the gallon, it probably has a ten- or twelve-gallon gas tank. That gas tank is all a Honda Civic needs; it doesn't need a huge gas tank.

Perhaps later on, that young man has become so good at delivering those papers on that route that the managers say, "We want to put you in charge of a whole district. In fact, we will give you a delivery truck to use to deliver the many bundles of newspapers."

The delivery truck happens to be a diesel truck with a 50-gallon tank. That young man went from driving a Civic with a little ten-gallon tank to a diesel truck with a 50-gallon tank.

Soon he gets so good with his deliveries the management said, "You have become so good at doing your job that we want to put you on the road. You will be delivering papers intrastate, and you will be driving a semi." That semi has two 50-gallon tanks, so he now has 100 gallons of fuel.

Perhaps he will go into even bigger business, and he will need a plane to fly back and forth from state to state. The plane he flies has a 300- or 400-gallon tank. Business gets so good that he gets a huge Federal Express or UPS Boeing 747 which carries about 70,000 or 80,000 gallons of fuel. That young man has come a long way from a ten-gallon Honda Civic to an 80,000-gallon Boeing 747! It all depends on a person's opportunity and the influence he needs to have.

Some junior-high age, high-school age, or college-age young people want to have some experience, so they try to pray down a "Boeing 747" when all they need at this time is a bicycle. It's not about how much you have compared to how much someone else has. That is one reason why I worry about those who have experiences. Certainly experiences can be wonderful motivators and provokers to get the power of God, but your experience will not be the same as Brother Hyles' lying on his father's grave and begging God for fresh oil.

Many people have gone to the gravesite of Brother Hyles' father in Italy, Texas, and they have fallen on their faces on that same gravesite, hoping for the same happening or experience. In most cases, nothing happened to those people. Some may have had something happen, but that is their personal business.

People stand by Brother Hyles' crypt in Memory Lane, put their hand against the marble, and say, "Oh, God, do it again!" I have done that also, but the ground didn't shake, and the crypt didn't open. To be sure, if it had, I would've gotten out of there! (I'll be honest, I don't want to have that kind of experience. I don't want the graves opening up unless I'm going up with them in the Rapture! When I prayed at the crypt of my father-in-law, I wasn't trying to copy an experience, but I am trying to get the power of God in my life for what I have to do.

Consider this scenario: A person gets saved and begins coming to church. He then learns how to dress right. He learns to discontinue bad habits like smoking, and he gets rid of the beer in his refrigerator. He cancels the HBO cable television service. Maybe he gets asked to be a greeter or a bus worker. He says, "How can I do that? How can I be a part of the First Baptist Church team?"

He can be, but he will now need a larger capacity. He will need a bigger teaspoon and a bigger measuring cup because God is going to give him more responsibility. He becomes faithful in that responsibility, which, by the way, is one of the ways to increase more volume. Even more responsibility comes his way.

Perhaps he is promoted from being a worker on a bus route to being a captain. Again he wonders, "How can I do that? God, I don't believe it! First Baptist Church wants me to be a bus captain!"

> *I need Thee, O, I need Thee;*
> *Every hour I need Thee!*

He prays, "Father, increase Your measuring cup. I yield to You the best I know how. Father, I don't know how I can do it. Please crucify my old flesh. I can't do it in the energy of the flesh, but I can do it with Your Spirit. Oh God, give me a bigger measuring cup. I need more of Your Spirit. Help me to help those who cross my path as Jesus would if He were in my shoes."

God likes that kind of attitude, and God says, "I'm going to give him a bigger measuring cup." By the power of the Holy Spirit, he receives a bigger measuring cup, which is, in simple terms, greater spiritual influence. After he becomes the bus captain, the route grows and grows. Soon he says to the bus director, "I need another bus." When he gets that bus, he goes to God and says, "What have I done? Oh, God, help me! I need more now."

Maybe he starts dating and falls in love, gets engaged, and gets married. He needs a bigger measuring cup. When the children come, he needs an even bigger measuring cup. An opportunity comes to sing in the choir, and he says, "Wow! They want me to sing in the choir? What an opportunity! How can I do that?"

Yes, singing in the choir is a wonderful opportunity. He now needs a bigger measuring cup than he did when he sat in the audience during all of the services. As a choir member, God is using him to help influence people to prepare their hearts for the preaching of the Word of God.

Maybe a day comes when he is asked to be an assistant pastor, so he says, "Whatever you want me to do," but he thinks, "God wants me to be an assistant pastor? Does He know what He's asking for? How can I do that?"

What he needs again is a bigger measuring cup. As this individual's influence grows, children come along, reach adulthood, marry, and grandchildren come along. When opportunities come, a bigger measuring cup is needed.

Since February 6, 2001, First Baptist Church of Hammond has needed more of a filling. Why? A man who was incredibly filled and full of the Holy Spirit of God was taken. That loss required all of us to step it up a little bit and say, "God, I must do my part. I must win souls. I must go to the bus route. I must be faithful to that Sunday school class. I will sing in the choir. I'm going to do more and more."

How can you do it all? You need to say, "Heavenly Father, I come to You right now the best I know how. I yield to You, Father. Would You crucify my old, sinful flesh? Would You pour out Your Spirit upon me in a mighty way? I want to be a part of continuing the legacy of Brother Hyles. I know I cannot do that without You. Would You increase the measuring cup that You use to pour out that Spirit? Help me to help those You bring across my path as Jesus would if He were in my shoes." Pray that prayer or one like it many, many times a day.

How do you get that measuring size increased?

II.
Love Righteousness, and Hate Iniquity

An amazing statement is found in Hebrews 1:8 and 9 that is copied from Psalm 45. It is an amazing conversation between God the Father and God the Son, and we are allowed to eavesdrop. They are discussing the fact that Christ, the Son of God, has had such a tremendous influence; in fact, more than anybody who has ever lived. God the Father is explaining to His own Son, Jesus, why He will have so much more influence than anyone would ever have. God told Jesus He was so much better than the angels or any human being as far as quality or worth.

Hebrews 1:8 and 9 explain why Jesus received influence. *"But unto the Son he* [God the Father] *saith, Thy throne, O God, is for ever and ever: a sceptre of righteousness is the sceptre of thy kingdom. Thou hast loved righteousness, and hated iniquity; therefore God, even thy God, hath anointed thee with the oil of gladness above thy fellows."*

The *"oil of gladness"* is a beautiful term, referring to the Holy Spirit. That statement is found only twice in the Bible. The Bible talks about the oil that ran down Aaron's beard and that is a picture of the anointing of the Holy Spirit. The priests would anoint a person with the olive oil on their head because it symbolized the anointing of the Holy Spirit. When a man became a king, he was anointed in the same way, showing that God had set him aside as an ordained, appointed man who was anointed by the Spirit of God for this task. When a man became a prophet, he too, was anointed. When a priest was ordained, he was also anointed with oil. Prophet, priest, and king were the three major offices of the Bible. Those who were in these positions had oil poured upon them because oil pictured the oil of gladness or the oil of influence or the oil of the Spirit of God or the Spirit of God.

God is saying to His Son, "You, Son, have been anointed with the Spirit of the Living God and the oil of gladness above your fellows and above everybody else for two reasons: (1) You love righteousness, and (2) You hate iniquity." To the person who would like to increase the portion God gives to him it's really quite simple: love right and hate wrong.

"What wrong or what kind of wrong?" you say.

The wrong you immediately thought of!

"Do you mean_____?" or "What about _____?"

Yes, that is exactly what I mean. If there is any question about hating wrong, the question comes down to this. How badly do you want to be filled with the Holy Spirit? If you even remotely wonder, "Would I have to give up _____?" yes, you probably would. If you can think of it or if it comes to mind, and your conscience provokes you, that is what God is referring to in these verses.

Specifically, the word *righteousness* means "equity or justice." God said, *"Thou hast loved righteousness...."* Righteousness is the love of seeing right done in every case. Loving something done rightly or loving someone being treated rightly is righteousness. Loving the right treatment

[123]

of those less fortunate than we are is righteousness. It is loving the right behavior in church.

Brother Hyles taught that most people think of justice in regard to how people treat them. Righteousness says, "I want others to be treated just like I would like to be treated." Righteousness is nothing more than applying the golden rule to relationships. Not only is it doing unto others as you would like them to do to you, but also it is the desire to see others treated as you would want done to you.

At times, I am told stories about how someone has been mistreated. May I ask, "Would you have gotten as upset if the same incident happened to a friend of yours or to someone else you know? Would you be coming to my office if another person's son got injured at school? If another's son got into a fight at school, would you come to me?"

Suppose you witnessed a situation you felt should be brought to my attention. Would you say, "Brother Schaap, my children were not involved in any way, but I want you to know that I witnessed a certain incident. I am disturbed by what I saw, and I'm as concerned about this situation as if it were my own son or daughter involved."

That kind of attitude shows righteousness. Righteousness says, "I want everybody treated rightly, and I mean everybody, not just me." In fact, righteousness goes beyond the second mile and says, "If I had a choice, I'd rather you be treated right than I."

Are you as happy when someone else gets a raise as you are when you do? Are you as happy when somebody else gets promoted as you would be if you had been? Is it as important at work that somebody else get treated as right as you would want to be treated? Righteousness is saying in every situation of life, "I want everything and everyone treated in a right manner."

If Jesus were asked how He had unlimited power, He

would no doubt say, "I love right. There's a right way and a wrong way to do something. I love it when right is done."

The admonition is also given that we are to "hate iniquity." What exactly is iniquity? Some would think, "anything that's wrong," but iniquity is a deeper word than that definition. Let me explain the difference between the words *iniquity* and *sin*.

If I have a barrier or a line and if I choose to cross that line, I have transgressed. The word *trans* means "over" or "across," and *gress* means "to step or walk." *Transgress* means, "I have crossed over the line." Literally, that is what *sin* means. Sin is a transgression or "overstepping" or "crossing over the line" of the law.

God says, *"Thou shalt not...."* An individual breaks that law by crossing the line which is sin. Technically, that sin is not iniquity. I call iniquity that which makes an individual determined and say, "It's okay for me to cross that line." Iniquity is the pride, the arrogance, the self-will, and the self-justification that says, "You may cross that line." The person **sins** when he crosses the line, but the **iniquity** in his heart is what justifies his crossing the line. That's why a long time before a man crosses a line, a long process of wicked thinking has been going on. Sin is simply a manifestation of the iniquity in a person's heart. I was born in sin, but I was conceived in iniquity. Nine months before I was born in sin, iniquity was already forming in me.

Iniquity is the pride and self-will that justifies wrong. Iniquity is the inner jury or judge that declares it permissible for a person to sin. Iniquity is the self permission. Let me explain. I hate sin, but do you know there's no place in the Bible where it says that I am supposed to hate sin? I checked carefully. Certainly, you and I know we should hate sin, but nowhere does it specifically state that in the Bible. Rather, the Bible says we are supposed to hate iniquity because if we hate iniquity, we will be light-years away from sin.

Many a person hates sin, but he doesn't mind flirting with it in his heart. I do not believe a person really wants to commit adultery, but he doesn't mind looking, thinking, or wondering. That process is iniquity. The Lord Jesus Christ hates iniquity; He hates what is in a man's heart that justifies his right to break God's laws.

If we would hate the pride that brings the sin, we would not sin. If isn't sin alone that God hates; He hates that which people use to justify breaking God's laws. Yes, we should hate sin, but I call that shallow—a kindergarten level of hate. Add to that the collegiate level of hating the pride that says it's okay to sin. Those who love things being done right will hate it when people justify doing that which is wrong.

How can I get that bigger measuring cup, Lord? "I love it when people are treated right," He says. "I love it when things are done rightly. I love righteousness, and I hate it that anybody would think it is fine to justify breaking one of My Father's laws. My God said, 'Thou shalt not,...' so what gives anyone the right to justify breaking that command? I hate iniquity."

How's your measuring cup? Do you hate sin and iniquity? Do you hate dirty videos and the attitude that says it is fine to bring them into your house? Pride says, "I think I'll go ahead and watch a video. It won't hurt me!" Do you hate cigarettes and hate the attitude that a person has the right to do with his body as he pleases? If you are saved, according to I Corinthians 6:19 and 20, your body is the temple of the Holy Spirit. *"What? know ye not that your body is the temple of the Holy Ghost which is in you, which ye have of God, and ye are not your own? For ye are bought with a price: therefore glorify God in your body, and in your spirit, which are God's."* It hurts me when I know I have iniquity in my heart.

Usually one doesn't realize he has iniquity until after he has sinned, and then he says, "Oh, how could I have done that?" How? Because he justified the iniquity. God is after that iniquity in our hearts.

How's your measuring cup? If you are content with a thimble full, then go ahead and love your sin of listening to rock 'n roll, drinking, swearing, wearing immodest clothing, or taking part in mixed swimming, but don't expect to have the mighty baptism of the power of God and the influence you need to be a part of changing a wicked, dying, and cursed world to righteousness. This world doesn't just need Christians to stop sinning; it needs born-again Christians to say, "I don't want sin in my life nor do I want iniquity, and I surely don't want to justify it."

For me, the most painful thing that happens when I sin is not that I realize I sinned, but that I justified my sin. Who am I to give myself permission to break an eternal law of a holy God? A careful reading of Psalm 51, that powerful chapter of repentance from David after he had committed adultery with Bathsheba, reveals that he confessed both the sin or transgression of the law of God prohibiting adultery AND the iniquity within him that justified the sin.

III.
Magnify the Words of God?

There is another reason that Jesus received a larger measure of God's Spirit. John 3:34 says, *"For he whom God hath sent speaketh the words of God: for God giveth not the Spirit by measure unto him."* This verse is saying that the size of the measure is determined by the degree to which you magnify God's Word. We speak far too much about our opinions, our views, and our thoughts. Instead, let's follow the advice of the songwriter when he wrote,

Let's talk about Jesus, / The King of kings is He,
The Lord of Lords supreme thru all eternity,
The great I am the way, the Truth, the Life, the Door;
Let's talk about Jesus more and more.

Every time Jesus opened His mouth, He spoke the Word of God. When you start making the Bible part of your vocabulary, God will be impressed.

"Brother Schaap, do you mean actually talk about the Bible?"

Yes! God wrote a Book, and He wants us to talk about His Book. Joshua 1:8a says, *"This book of the law shall not depart out of thy mouth; but thou shalt meditate therein day and night."* Let's talk about Jesus. Let's talk about His Book. Let's magnify the old King James. We can have the power of God if we focus on His Word. There's far too much talk about football, baseball, basketball, and other sports. I am not against talking about these subjects, and I am not suggesting we stop talking about them. Sometimes a person's sports knowledge can be a delightful, wonderful introduction to get out the Gospel or to have a light conversation with some buddies.

The person who gives 100 percent of his time to talking about the things of this world, never talking about the Bible, never mentioning a Bible verse, or never reading the Bible shows that he is out of balance. That person will not have the mighty baptism of the power of God unless he makes the Bible the centerpiece of his mouth.

We can discuss business, decisions, money, finances, marriage, and a thousand other things, but the Bible should be a regular, frequent subject in our conversation. If it is not, then we need to pray, "Oh God, the best I know how, I yield to You, Father. I need You. Crucify my flesh that's full of iniquity, and fill me with the Spirit of God, please." If that is the only time you talk about Him, God says, "Give him another thimble full."

IV.
Protect Your Own Spirit

Another way a person can increase his measure is found in II King 2 which tells the story of Elijah and Elisha. At this time, Elijah was depressed and going through a tough time. As my wife and I were discussing this chapter one day, she pointed out a great truth. She asked, "Did you ever realize what God gave Elijah when he was depressed? God gave him a friend—Elisha."

There are times when I believe Christians become too isolated. Isolation brings depression. The depressed person climbs into a hole or hides in a shelter when he needs some friends and a social life. God gave Elijah a friend, a buddy named Elisha who went everywhere with him.

When I think of friends, I think of Mrs. Marlene Evans and some of the dear ladies who were her good friends. I think those ladies helped keep her alive a longer time. At some difficult times in her life, God gave her friends.

I know Brother Hyles' best friend was Mrs. Hyles. I think God prolonged the life of Brother Hyles because he had a friend in his wife. God gives friends to people going through tough times.

After Elisha had served Elijah, the time came when Elijah said to Elisha, "God told me it's getting close to the time I've got to leave. Is there anything I can do for you?" I can almost hear the conversation in my mind.

"Yes, there is."

"Name it!"

"These many months I have been watching you. I love

[129]

your spirit. [Not the Holy Spirit, but Elijah's spirit.] I like your attitude about situations. I like the way you look at life."

"What would you like, Elisha?"

"When you leave, I'd like to have a double portion of *your* spirit." [Notice that Elisha did not ask for a double portion of the Holy Spirit; he asked for a double portion of Elijah's spirit.]

Did you ever wonder why God performed twice as many miracles using Elisha? In the 15 or so specific stories about Elisha, you will never find him out of sorts. He is one of those rare characters with an even disposition. Elijah, however, did get out of sorts. Elijah went through a huge valley of despair on at least two occasions. God used him to perform 6 miracles. Elisha never went down into that state of depression or despair, at least none are recorded. God used him to perform 12 miracles. He did indeed have a double portion of that incredible attitude and spirit of Elijah. Our word *attitude* is not found in the Bible, but our word *attitude* is a very good synonym for the word *spirit*.

You might wonder, "What does the story of Elijah and Elisha have to do with the Spirit of God?" Because the Holy Spirit can only work through you according to the health of your spirit. The Holy Spirit works through your own spirit. How would you like to work with a grump all of the time? You grumble a prayer, "God, fill me," and He says, "Yuck. Who would want to work through you? Give him a little thimble full."

Have you ever wondered why Brother Hyles had so much spirit? The one characteristic about Brother Hyles that was so incredible was his spirit. Do you remember how he used to say, "I don't live down where you folks do. I live up here above the clouds." You say, "Oh, I wish I could be like Brother Hyles." I believe anyone can do it. You purpose to live above the clouds, and the Spirit of God comes and baptizes you with a greater measure.

When my daughter was a high school cheerleader, I attended a soccer game at which she was cheering. One of our boys accidentally kicked the ball into the wrong goal. Oh, that player felt stupid. The coach pulled him aside to calm him. All of the players and all of the cheerleaders were saying, "Oh, no!"

I called to my daughter and motioned her to come to where I was sitting. "Jaclynn," I said, "this is why they pay you the big money. This is your golden opportunity. This is exactly why we have cheerleaders. It's not to get a date with the cutest guy on the opposing team. Now, is your time to shine! Your team is depressed; their spirit has been broken because of a dumb mistake, and their attitude is down in the gutter. Now, you girls get out there on the sidelines and show everyone that you have earned the right to be a cheer- leader."

The cheerleaders ran back to their places in front of the crowd, and began to cheer and cheer and cheer, and they pumped up the spirits of our players. That is exactly what the purpose of cheerleading is—to generate a good spirit.

When you generate a good spirit inside of you, the Holy Spirit says, "Would you like a little more of Me? I can work through a person with a happy spirit and a good attitude."

When you sit in church with a closed spirit and crossed arms, a preacher cannot yell loudly enough to get through because the bars of your spirit are closed against the preach- ing. When you close off your spirit, no one can get through. Open your spirit, so the preaching can get through. If you open your spirit, God's Spirit can work through you. You can close off your spirit so much that God says, "I can't get through to your closed spirit."

Perhaps your spirit is wounded because of marital problems or because of difficulties with your children. That wounded spirit you have can be like a cobra in a bad mood. If somebody comes around you, you hiss, "Shut up!"

I was at Hyles-Anderson College not too long after we said goodbye to Brother Hyles. As I walked past a student, I said, "Hello."

He said, "Don't you know I'm sad?"

I wanted to say, "Well, you think I'm not?"

To be sure, I was sorry for the person's grief and unhappiness, but what he needed was an open spirit so God could help him. His wounded spirit of grief and sadness was not allowing God's Spirit to help him or anyone who crossed his path.

We have discussed four very practical, easy-to-understand ways that every Christian can use to get God to increase the size of the measure that He uses to pour out the Holy Spirit into a person's life. Jesus never had a measure. He hated iniquity, loved righteousness, and every time He opened His mouth, he spoke the Word of God. *"Never man spake like this man,"* was said about Him. (John 7:46b) What a Spirit He possessed because He was the Spirit!

I helped crucify that Man. I joined in the pounding of the nails into His hands, so I helped to crucify Him. That Man was the Son of God. What a Spirit He possessed! Can you imagine how He must have laid down his life? I can almost hear Him say, "Go ahead. Pound the nails. Go ahead. I forgive you." What an attitude! No wonder He had an unlimited reserve of power, and that Spirit is exactly what you could have if you qualified.

CHAPTER SEVEN

Protecting the Fire

■   ■   ■

I Thessalonians 5:16-22 says, *"Rejoice evermore. Pray without ceasing. In every thing give thanks: for this is the will of God in Christ Jesus concerning you. Quench not the Spirit. Despise not prophesyings. Prove all things; hold fast that which is good. Abstain from all appearance of evil."*

In I Thessalonians 5 is found a series of short, punchy verses. Starting in verse 16, the next three verses say, *"Rejoice evermore. Pray without ceasing. In every thing give thanks...."* Those three verses are located in front of the words, *"Quench not the Spirit."* Three more verses follow: *"Despise not prophesyings. Prove all things; Abstain from all appearance of evil."* The central verse in this series of instructions is, *"Quench not the Spirit."*

English students know that when they write a paragraph, they usually have what is called a topic sentence. Each paragraph supposedly addresses one topic or one idea. Whether you write a letter or an essay, a paragraph generally consists of one subject with a topic sentence to introduce that subject. As most would know, the topic sentence is not always the first sentence. Commonly it is, but somewhere in each paragraph, a topic sentence should be found.

In the same way, this series of seven short verses form a paragraph with the topic sentence being the middle verse, *"Quench not the Spirit."* In a previous chapter, the subject of grieving the Spirit was addressed, but this verse is not addressing grieving the Spirit. The word *quench* is the word *extinguish,* just like a fireman uses a fire extinguisher to put out a fire.

This verse is a command. If you will notice, the Bible doesn't say, "your spirit." In this verse, the word *Spirit* has a capital *S*. The King James Bible translators were very careful to capitalize the word *Spirit* in the New Testament when it referred to the Holy Spirit. Thus, every time the word *Spirit* has a capital *S*, that always refers to the Holy Spirit.

In the Old Testament, however, the word *spirit* has to be used in context to discover whether or not the Scripture is referring to God's Spirit or man's spirit. Of course, this verse is saying don't quench or extinguish or blow out or put out the fire of the Holy Spirit.

Proverbs 16:32 says, *"He that is slow to anger is better than the mighty; and he that ruleth his spirit than he that taketh a city."* In this verse, the word *spirit* has a small *s*, but that doesn't necessarily indicate whether or not it is man's spirit or God's spirit. The context is very plain. It says, *"...he that ruleth **his** spirit,"* and that is referring to man.

The key text I want to focus on in this chapter is Proverbs 25:28, which says, *"He that hath no rule over his own spirit is like a city that is broken down, and without walls."* About whose spirit are the words "his own spirit," speaking? Obviously, the verse is not referring to God's Spirit; it is referring to man's spirit.

In the previous chapter, the importance of a person's spirit and how it plays a role with the Holy Spirit was discussed. The Holy Spirit resides in man's spirit.

Let me illustrate. Picture in your mind, if you will, two

men standing side-by-side, shoulder to shoulder, facing in the same direction representing my spirit. If the two men are representing my closed spirit and if I am representing the Holy Spirit, I cannot get through to my spirit by trying to push between them. My inability to force my way through "my closed spirit" illustrates how the Holy Spirit has a hard time getting through me to do His work.

What else does this illustration mean? Perhaps the Holy Spirit is having a hard time getting through to a person's closed spirit during the preaching of the Word of God. Going back to my illustration; the Holy Spirit wants to get through with the Word of God to the sinners, but He cannot get through a preacher's closed spirit. The Word of God can't get through either. Why? Because if the person's spirit is closed, the Holy Spirit can't get through. If I, as a preacher, attempt to preach with a closed spirit, my spirit will prevent the Holy Spirit from getting through with the message of the Word of God.

Have you ever had a hard time witnessing to someone, and you felt like you were talking to a cardboard box? If your spirit was closed, you may have found it difficult to share the spiritual truth with a sinner.

However, let's suppose I open my spirit, and in having an open spirit, the Holy Spirit can get through my spirit. Suppose though, I cannot get through the sinner's spirit because his spirit is closed. In order to get the Word of God or the Spirit of God to work through me to another person, we both have to have open spirits.

If an unsaved person has his spirit open to me, then I can take the Holy Spirit or Word of God straight through. The Spirit of God can then take what is preached and use it to help work inside of that person and change his life.

The tool that the Holy Spirit uses to change a person's life is the Word of God. That tool is one reason why preaching is so important. Titus 1:3 says, *"manifested his word through preaching."* God has ordained preaching to manifest His Word. It is from the preaching of the Word of God that people will learn most of their Bible. Certainly, a diligent student of the Bible might learn a lot of Bible from personal study, and he should; however, the bottom line is that God knows the average Christian will learn most of his Bible through the preaching of the Word of God.

The reason why the listener has the Word of God in him and the Holy Spirit can work inside of him is because his spirit is open. The preacher's spirit was also open. There was a free flow of the Spirit of God, thus the message got through. If the listener's spirit is closed, and/or the preacher's spirit is closed, the message cannot get through, no matter how much pizzazz the preacher has. Nothing can or will happen because the listener's spirit is closed, and/or the preacher's spirit is closed.

The Bible says that the secret to having the Holy Spirit working in your life is your own spirit. *"He that hath no rule over his own spirit is like a city that is broken down, and without walls."* What does that verse mean? A broken-down city means the city behind the walls has nothing internally worth protecting. For whatever reason, it is a derelict city.

If I say, "Holy Spirit, help me to open my spirit," my spirit is now being controlled. If I have rule over my spirit, then as a pastor, I can get out the message. However, if you as a listener do not have the rule over your spirit, I am still prevented from helping you internally because you have no control over your spirit.

The Bible says if I don't have control over my spirit internally, I'm in a predicament. I'm like a city that is broken down, decayed, and spoiled; the buildings are dilapidated and need to be refurbished. There's nothing inside the city worth salvaging. *"Without walls"* means that I have no protection. Even if it looks like I'm protected by a closed spirit, I'm not protected. The person who doesn't have control over his spirit is his own man doing his own thing, and he is probably going to get into a lot of trouble.

That definition describes a teenager who doesn't want to listen to his parents or a teenager who listens to the world's music. This verse also describes a teenager who looks at pornography or watches cable programs with HBO and Showtime. It also characterizes a deacon or a preacher watching the same kind of programs. If I don't have control over my own spirit, I am a city broken down without anything internally worth protecting, and I have no protection on the outside because I have no walls around my spirit.

How do I control my spirit? Let me explain by using a candle to represent the Holy Spirit. A lit candle represents the Holy Spirit's illumination in a Christian's life. In I Thessalonians 5:16-22, the Bible is teaching that God gives the Christian six ways to protect or to rule his own spirit. The Holy Spirit can work through the person who will rule his own spirit. If I don't rule my own spirit, the Holy Spirit cannot work through me. So, God says I hold the key to the Holy Spirit's fire not going out in my life.

Some of you say, "I lack comfort. I'm grieving. Some people seem to have all this grace when they go through times of need. Why don't I?" The answer is simple. You have not because you have not gained control of your own spirit.

"Brother Schaap, what does it mean to control my own spirit?" It is possessing these six guardians of the Holy Spirit's fire. The guards fortify my spirit, so I can keep the fire of the Holy Spirit lit and alive and burning in my life; that means the Holy Spirit is working in me and through me to help others.

How does a person, *"Quench not the Spirit"*? Again the

answer is simple. By protecting my own spirit, then His Spirit is not quenched. The Bible says that if I do not have control over my own spirit, the six guardians are not shielding me. Enemies can blow out my fire because I have no protection or control over my spirit.

You ask, "Why don't you do something about it?" When I have no protection, all I can do is hold the flame and hope it doesn't go out. My spirit is powerless or unprotected.

Even with having a guardian on each side, the candle can still be blown out by the enemy. If I add another guardian, with some work the candle can still be blown out. If I have all six guardians, however, my fire is safe. That is why some Christians' candles go out, but others don't. Maintain your guardians so the devil can't bother you.

In my own power, if I try to protect the fire with my own spirit, I can't. My spirit's job is to provide a habitation for the Holy Spirit, but if I don't have control over my spirit, then I am an easy prey or an easy victim for that which will blow out my candle. When you are at this state of vulnerability, sometimes you don't even know if the candle is out because you have been so distracted. You have so ignored your spirit that you quite possibly do not even know your candle has been extinguished.

The Devil (or enemies of your spirit) will attack you when in your weakness you don't even know your candle is out. Many "pretend" Christians walk around with the Holy Spirit quenched. I am not saying those Christians are not saved. *"Quench not the Spirit"* does not mean that the Spirit of God has left a Christian. No one can be unsaved once he is saved. This verse is referring to the illumination.

What is illumination? When a person reads the Bible, it becomes clear. The illuminating power of the Holy Spirit helps a person see the Word of God. I don't mean a person can merely see the words; The Holy Spirit, as the Author of the Words of God, illuminates or sheds light on those words spiritually so they can be understood.

That illumination also applies to preaching. When you're listening to preaching and suddenly you understand the concept, you might say, "Oh, I get what he's talking about. I need to walk the aisle. He got to me." When the Spirit of God sheds light on the preaching and when it made sense, the listener was convicted. The Holy Spirit shed light and opened up the closed compartments in the listener's heart.

I want the Spirit of God to shed light on the Word of God when I read it, to shed light on the preaching of the Word of God when I hear it preached, and to shed light on the teaching of the Word of God when I hear it taught; therefore, I need the illumination of the Holy Spirit to guide my way. Psalm 119:105 says, *"Thy word is a lamp unto my feet, and a light unto my path."* *"Thy Word"* is the Word of God, of course; but Who makes the Word of God light up your path and be a lamp? The Spirit of God does. A person can use the Bible all he wants, but if he doesn't have the Spirit of God illuminating him on the inside, he cannot understand the Words of God. I Corinthians 2:9-14 states, *"But as it is written, Eye hath not seen, nor ear heard, neither have entered into the heart of man, the things which God hath prepared for them that love him. But God hath revealed them unto us by his Spirit: for the Spirit searcheth all things, yea, the deep things of God. For what man knoweth the things of a man, save the spirit of man which is in him? even so the things of God knoweth no man, but the Spirit of God. Now we have received, not the spirit of the world, but the spirit which is of God; that we might know the things that are freely given to us of God. Which things also we speak, not in the words which man's wisdom teacheth, but which the Holy Ghost teacheth; comparing spiritual things with spiritual. But the natural man receiveth not the things of the Spirit of*

God: for they are foolishness unto him: neither can he know them, because they are spiritually discerned.." Notice the words in bold type. The Words of God are words chosen by the Holy Spirit of God, and these words are foolishness to those who do not have God's Spirit to illuminate them to the reader or hearer.

Every false religion or cult in the United States of America is built on the Word of God. Mormons, Jehovah's Witnesses, and Catholics all use the Bible. Even the Muslims admit that the Bible is an exceptionally good book written by a great prophet. Still, the Bible can be the most dangerous book in the world to an un-illuminated person. The student of the Bible needs the illumination of the Holy Spirit. The problem is, the Mormons don't have the Holy Spirit inside them to illuminate the Word of God. When they read the Book, they cannot understand it; it is a foreign book to them. That is why they fabricated an entire system of heresy and damnation. Their heresy uses the Bible against the very Author of the Bible because they don't have the Author of the Bible inside them illuminating the Words of God.

Christian, you're just as dangerous as a Mormon without the illumination of the Holy Spirit. Did you ever notice how many Mormons are Baptist converts? Did you ever notice how many Jehovah's Witnesses are Baptist converts? When you pin them down, you will find many of them have been saved as they finally acknowledge, "Well, yeah, I was saved at Baptist camp when I was a little kid." You may wonder and sometimes ask, "Whatever are you doing in this situation?" They got into a cult because they never got control of their own spirit or regarded the Spirit of God in them. The Spirit of God was extinguished, just like a candle is blown out. Those people did not control nor protect their spirits.

Let me show you how you can protect your own spirit. In I Thessalonians 5, the Bible lists the six guardians of my spirit, which automatically makes them the guardians of the Holy Spirit. Man's spirit is the gateway through which God's Spirit works. If a person does not have control of his spirit, then the Holy Spirit's illumination will be extinguished and that Christian will be defenseless. He will lose the emphasis or illumination or the power of the Holy Spirit working inside of him.

1. *"Rejoice evermore."* (I Thessalonians 5:16) What is this verse saying? *"Rejoice evermore,"* means "eternally rejoice." It means constantly, without ceasing, never stopping, but forever rejoicing. It also means finding your joy in things eternal.

Let's go back to February 6, 2001, when God took Brother Hyles to Heaven. What did not change when Brother Hyles died? Depending how you answer that determines whether or not you have your joy. If your life was built only on the presence of a particular personality behind a pulpit, you became a very sad person when Brother Hyles went to Heaven. Certainly, it was not wrong to be sad. Brother Hyles had a very large influence on many people's lives as he taught the Bible. Though I miss him very much and I grieve over him, my joy was not built on him. Neither is my joy built on whether or not you show up at church on Sunday.

My joy is built on that which cannot change. What's the difference between "joy" and "happiness"? *Happiness* comes from the word *happening*, and it's what happens externally outside of your spirit. *Joy* is what's going on inside.

Remember the words of that song you sang in children's church?

I have the joy, joy, joy, joy, / Down in my heart,
Down in my heart, / Down in my heart, / I have the joy....

[141]

If the joy has left your heart, it's because your joy was built on that which was temporary or that which could change.

The truth that Brother Hyles preached is eternal. That is why I can accept everything Brother Hyles gave men that didn't change. For instance, Brother Hyles wrote a book entitled, *Meet the Holy Spirit*. The truths in the pages of that book haven't changed at all. The concepts he taught were built on the Bible. Brother Hyles also wrote a book called, *Exploring Prayer with Jack Hyles*. Every person should read it. Once again, the truths found in that book do not change even though the author's state changed. His pain-filled body was changed like unto His glorious body. He no longer has back pain, but the truths that he taught me have not changed. My hope and my joy are built on the truth that never changes. What did not change when Brother Hyles died? If you are saved, your name is still written in Heaven. That's good news! Everyone whose name is written in Heaven is supposed to rejoice!

If you want to be protected, Christian, you need to have joy down in your heart. My first line of defense against the enemy is, *"Rejoice evermore."*

What else did not change? The Bible is still the eternal Word of God. Do you know what is wrong with those Christians who say, "I know this is true, but it just doesn't work for me." I know it does not work because they do not have the illuminating power. Their fire went out. Get your candle lit, and keep it lit! You get your candle lit and keep it lit by getting joy in your heart.

You find your joy in things eternal. Don't let circumstances determine whether or not you have joy. If you will get excited about things that cannot change then when things change that you cannot control, you will not lose your joy because it is built on that which is eternal. When you lose your joy, you start changing those things which you can change which never should be changed.

2. *"Pray without ceasing."* (I Thessalonians 5:17) Does this verse mean that I am supposed to be on my knees all the time? No, of course not! *"Pray without ceasing"* means "don't ever give up on prayer."

If you say, "Well, I tried that and it didn't work," keep on praying.

Just keep on praying (till light breaks) through,
The Lord will answer, (will answer) you;
God keeps His promise (His Word is) true,
Just keep on praying till light breaks through.

These are the wonderful words of an old song. Don't ever give up on prayer! Pray without ever stopping your confidence that God hears your prayers.

"Pray without ceasing" does not mean your mouth is moving all of the time or you are on your knees all of the times. The verse does not mean you are always in an attitude of prayer. In fact, there is no such thing as an attitude of prayer. A person either prays or he doesn't pray.

Even if God doesn't answer all my prayers the way I want, I know that if I don't quit on prayer and if I don't give up on prayer, I have a better chance of keeping that candle lit inside my life. The moment I give up on prayer and prayer sits down, I have just lost one of my major defenders against the enemy. The verse is saying that when you pray, don't ever give up on the power of prayer.

3. *"In every thing give thanks."* (I Thessalonians 5:18a) The first word of that is verse is *in*. The verse does not begin with the word *for*; it begins with the word *in*.

God says, "Do you want to keep the candle lit? Do you want to have the Spirit of the Living God burning deep inside you? If so, then, *'In every thing give thanks.'* "

[143]

Even if you don't feel thankful, say, "Thank You!" God says, "You will learn to have gratitude by giving thanks in everything."

One of the most remarkable books I have ever read about giving thanks is *The Hiding Place* by Corrie ten Boom, a true story based on her life during World War II. Corrie ten Boom was a Dutch girl who lived with her family in the Netherlands during World War II when Germans occupied their land. Her family opened up their house as a safe house to hide Jewish people from the Nazis. Eventually the family was caught aiding the Jews, so they were deported to the concentration camps. She and her sister were sent to one; her father was sent to a different one.

In her book, she shares how she and her sister endured the horrific conditions of the Nazi prison camp. Hundreds of women were stuffed inside dormitory rooms with rows and rows of beds and barely enough space to live. Their beds were like pens with straw matting that was infested with lice and fleas, so disease ran rampant.

Corrie's sister had managed to smuggle in a Bible, which was considered contraband. They were terrified they would get caught, so they did not take it out of hiding very often. Sometimes the Germans would even pay somebody to spy on the other prisoners and report on their activities. The two saved sisters were concerned because they could not get out the Gospel. They believed the only way they would survive the Nazi terrorism was through reading and studying the Word of God, praying, finding other believers with whom to fellowship, and encouraging others to get saved. The two sisters wanted to be a testimony.

The ten Booms began to pray, "Oh God, we need to find some way to keep these guards from seeing we have a Bible. You know if they see it, they will confiscate it, and we'll lose our strength and our only resource. We need to keep our

Bible." They prayed and prayed.

The guards had always walked up and down the rows, checking the prisoners. Four or five women were cramped together into a bunk-bed-type area. The guards walked back and forth through these areas, looking for anything with which they could pester the captives.

Without any announcement, the guards stopped inspecting the dormitory which the ten Boom sisters occupied. The ladies had suffered a lot of afflictions, but that had never stopped the presence of the guards. With no guards present, they began to take out the Bible and share the Words of God. Many of their fellow prisoners began to get saved. Large numbers began to gather unhindered for regular Bible studies.

The miracle for which the two sisters prayed continued; no guards inspected their dormitory. God had answered their prayers miraculously. They began to pray about their deplorable conditions. The flea and lice infestation was so bad the prisoners felt they couldn't survive. "God, please take away these fleas. We're about to go insane from the constant biting and itching."

One day Corrie and her sister were walking outside their dormitory prison, and overheard two guards talking. One asked, "Have you been in that dormitory?" She pointed to the dormitory where the ten Boom sisters were quartered.

"No, I won't go in there!"

"Why?"

"The fleas!"

The guard's words pierced Corrie ten Boom's heart. She said, "Thank You, God, not *for* the fleas, but *in* the fleas."

"All that time," Corrie said in her book, "the situation got so bad to me that I began to think my Christianity was weak. My prayer life seemingly wasn't going anywhere. I did not think that God heard me. My sister kept saying, 'Corrie, trust God. Don't give up. Keep on praying.'

I told God that the fleas were such an abomination that we literally thought we were going to go insane. When I heard that guard make that statement about the fleas, I returned to that dorm, dropped to my knees, and said, 'Thank You, God—not for the fleas, but thank You that in the fleas we have the freedom of the Gospel for which we prayed.' "

Like Corrie ten Boom, a person cannot be thankful *for* fleas, but he can be thankful *in* fleas. You cannot be thankful *for* the death of a loved one, but you can be thankful *in* it. I'm not thankful *for* the struggles and problems Christians have, but I can be thankful *in* them.

4. *"Despise not prophesyings."* (I Thessalonians 5:20) In this verse, the word *prophesying* is synonymous with the word *preaching. Despise* means "don't lowly esteem." Magnify, love, and anticipate preaching. Get excited, and say, "Amen" to the preaching of the Word of God.

God says, "To the degree a person magnifies preaching, I will give him a defense against the Devil." The Spirit of God says, "I love preaching, and if you like preaching like I do, I'll defend."

One of the best defenses we have against the enemy is to love preaching. We loved Brother Hyles' preaching all these years, so don't change that love for preaching. The verse does not say you have to love the preacher; it says to love the preaching. The verse does not say, "Despise not the prophesier"; it says, *"Despise not prophesyings."*

5. *"Prove all things; hold fast that which is good."* (I Thessalonians 5:21) This verse means *test all things.* It simply means "don't change Bibles." It simply means not to investigate other methods of soul winning. No! Hold fast to that which is true, firm, or tested. This verse means to use the tested methods.

For 41 years, we watched a man and a church meld and weld together to show the whole fundamental world how to do it. Bless God, let's not change one thing! We need the same Book, the same message, the same preaching, and the same music. Let's not change! Let's keep First Baptist Church the way you would want your grandchildren to have it some day.

In order to accomplish that goal, we need to keep the tested, proven methods. Let's not change the Bible. Let's not change the plan of salvation. Let's not change the Gospel. Let's not change the old Gospel songs. Let's not change the hymns of the faith. Let's not change the style. Let's not change the way it's sung. Let's keep the old, proven methods.

6. *"Abstain from all appearance of evil."* (I Thessalonians 5:22) To *abstain* means "to say no." Just say no to what? Say no to all appearance of evil. What is evil? Evil is when you're trying to hurt somebody else.

No matter in what form evil comes, always say, "No." Perhaps someone is criticizing another Christian or trying to hurt another individual with criticism. Say, "No," to hearing that garbage.

Suppose the evil comes in the form of a prayer request. "I'd like you to pray about a matter...." Just say, "No. I don't want to hear your gossip nor your criticism."

Perhaps the evil comes in the form of the printed page or a taped message. "Did you hear there's a tape out about such and such or a book has been written about ___?" Say, "NO! I don't want to hear the tape. I don't want to read the book. I don't want to hear about anyone who disagrees or doesn't approve. The only Person's approval I want is the Lord Jesus Christ.

My defense mechanisms are in place. My spirit is being ruled. I am sitting as a king with my spirit, and I have my sentries close by to protect my flame. I'm rejoicing evermore. I'm not going to give up on prayer. I'm going to give thanks *in* all things, not *for* them. I'm going to highly esteem or love preaching. I'm going to hold fast to the old proven methods. I'm going to abstain from all criticism or gossip no matter the source.

I double dog dare the enemy to blow out my candle. He won't be able to because I have the rule over my own spirit, and my path has illumination. Why? The Spirit of God is not being quenched because I am a protected Christian whose spirit is ruled by the six sentries of God. They are strong defenses to protect my spirit.

We need the Holy Spirit. I need Him. The Bible calls Him the Spirit of comfort. I can still hear the voice of Brother Hyles teaching that the word *Paraclete* means "the one called alongside to comfort," the One called alongside to help in time of need, the One called alongside to help during the difficulties and struggles. That One alongside bringing comfort is the Holy Spirit.

How much comfort is wasted, how much truth is never learned, how much influence is lost; all because we do not protect our spirits, and thus, we shut off the power of the Holy Spirit in our lives.

CHAPTER EIGHT

Qualifying for the Spirit

■   ■   ■

Luke 11:1-13 says, *"And it came to pass, that, as he was praying in a certain place, when he ceased, one of his disciples said unto him, Lord, teach us to pray, as John also taught his disciples. And he said unto them, When ye pray, say, Our Father which art in heaven, Hallowed be thy name. Thy kingdom come. Thy will be done, as in heaven, so in earth. Give us day by day our daily bread. And forgive us our sins; for we also forgive every one that is indebted to us. And lead us not into temptation; but deliver us from evil. And he said unto them, Which of you shall have a friend, and shall go unto him at midnight, and say unto him, Friend, lend me three loaves; For a friend of mine in his journey is come to me, and I have nothing to set before him? And he from within shall answer and say, Trouble me not: the door is now shut, and my children are with me in bed; I cannot rise and give thee. I say unto you, Though he will not rise and give him, because he is his friend, yet because of his importunity he will rise and give him as many as he needeth. And I say unto you, Ask, and it shall be given you; seek, and ye shall find; knock, and it shall be opened unto you. For every one that asketh receiveth; and he that seeketh findeth; and to him that knocketh it shall be opened. If a son shall ask bread of any of you that is a father, will he give him a stone?*

or if he ask a fish, will he for a fish give him a serpent? Or if he shall ask an egg, will he offer him a scorpion? If ye then, being evil, know how to give good gifts unto your children: how much more shall your heavenly Father give the Holy Spirit to them that ask him?"

This Scripture passage is what is commonly referred to as the model prayer or the Lord's Prayer. This is Jesus' instruction to His disciples as far as a recipe or a formula or an outline of how to pray.

Notice Luke 11:2, *"And he said unto them, When ye pray, say, Our Father...."* In my Bible, I circled the word, *Father*. In verse three, *"Give us day by day our daily bread,"* I circled the word, *bread*. I drew a line between the words *bread* and *Father*. The word *bread* is associated with the *Father*. When I am asking for my daily bread, I am speaking to the Father.

Verse five states, *"And he said unto them, Which of you shall have a friend, and shall go unto him at midnight, and say unto him, Friend...."* The word *friend* is introduced. Notice that the word *Friend* is capitalized. Of course, Jesus is speaking about deity. He is referring to a heavenly Friend. In my Bible, I have also circled the word *Friend*.

Verse five continues, *"...Friend, lend me three loaves."* The normal assumption would be that the *loaves* are bread. Thirty times in the Bible, the word *loaves* is found. In this particular passage, the Bible does not say, "Friend lend me some **bread**." Rather, it says, *"Friend, lend me three **loaves**."* In my Bible I have also circled the word *loaves*. I have also drawn a line between the words *loaves* and *Friend*.

In verse 11, *"If a son shall ask bread of any of you that is a father..."* I have circled the words *bread* and *father*, and I have connected the two words with a line.

Verse 13 continues, *"If ye then, being evil, know how to give good gifts unto your children: how much more shall your heavenly Father give the Holy Spirit to them that ask him?"* I have circled the words *Father* and *Holy Spirit*, and I have drawn a line between the words to connect them. From studying these verses, I have learned that if I want bread for myself, I address the Father or God as my Father. If I want loaves, I am supposed to address my Friend.

While teaching His disciples to pray, Jesus used analogies. The word *bread* is used when addressing physical, human needs. I need bread physically for food. Some use the word *bread* euphemistically as "money." *Bread* is used in the sense of needing some means to survive. Jesus is saying, "If you need help or need your physical needs cared for or if you need the wherewithal to live on a daily basis, you have the right to go to your Father and say, 'Father, I need some bread for me.' "

Likewise, that bread could also be referring to the Holy Spirit. We need the Holy Spirit for our personal needs. If we need comfort, the Holy Spirit can comfort us. If we need direction or insight, the Holy Spirit can give us direction and insight. If an individual needs the Holy Spirit for himself, he can go to his heavenly Father and say, 'Father, I need the Holy Spirit to help me here.' "

Certainly it is right and proper to talk to all three members of the Godhead. When Jesus prayed in the Bible, he talked to the Heavenly Father. He talked to the Heavenly Father because the Heavenly Father was in control.

When you need the Holy Spirit for personal help, just as you need bread, money, strength, energy, wisdom, guidance, or anything personally, go to the Heavenly Father and say, "Father, I need some things." The Bible says your Father is obligated to give them to you. In fact, your Father is very eager to give you things, including the Holy Spirit.

He says, "I'm more eager to give them to you than your earthly father is to give you a sandwich if you're hungry." Earthly fathers don't give their sons a stone if they want bread. If his child wants an egg, he doesn't give him a scorpion. If he wants a gift, his father tries to get it for him.

However, the Bible is speaking not only about bread in these verses; the Bible is talking also about loaves. Though bread and loaves sound similar, they are not. In 29 out of the 30 references to loaves in the Bible, the context is always in reference to another's needs, or it associates the loaves with the Holy Spirit. Only one reference is used otherwise; the Bible is speaking about waving loaves to God in a sacrificial offering.

In I Samuel 10, an unsaved Saul had just met Samuel and was told by the prophet to continue down the road. He was told he would meet three men who had three loaves, and Samuel said, *"And they will salute thee, and give thee two loaves of bread; which thou shalt receive of their hands."* (I Samuel 10:4)

Loaves in the Bible referred to the Holy Spirit being used to help someone in a time of need. Bread refers to my personal needs, and loaves refer to your needs. So, if I have a personal need and if I say, "Father, I have a personal need," or "I need the Holy Spirit to guide me and give me wisdom," or "I need your direction," or "I need a little extra help financially," or "Father, I need help," the Father is the One to whom I address my needs. He is obligated to take care of my needs.

However, if I see that someone else has a need, whether or not it's a financial need or a guidance need or a wisdom need or a knowledge need or a need that I can't supply, I then say, "They have loaves that they need." I don't go to my Father and get loaves. I go to my Friend and get loaves. I want to elaborate on this procedure because a person must qualify to get loaves.

In this chapter, I want to address the matter of qualifying for the Holy Spirit. Many are trying to get something when they have not earned the right to have it. It's just like a 14-year-old boy asking for the car keys. "You haven't earned the right, Son," Dad says.

"I know, but I'm a good driver."

"You may think you are the best driver in the world, but you haven't earned the right to have the car yet."

Just like a teenager has to qualify for a driver's license, there are certain things for which a person has to be qualified before he may have them. When I refer to qualifying for the Holy Spirit, I am not referring to whether or not a person receives the Holy Spirit. You receive the Holy Spirit of God the moment you receive Jesus Christ as your Saviour. It's instantaneous! The Bible says the Holy Spirit is actually the legal down payment that He makes assuring you that He will save you when He comes back.

Humans live in mortal bodies that are full of sin. In fact, the body is so full of sin that it will eventually die. The body grows old, or gets some fatal disease like cancer, and rots and dies. Why? The body dies because of sin! However, the Bible says that when I trusted Christ as my Saviour, God promised that not only would He take my soul to Heaven, but He would also redeem my body. He would also redeem all of His creation and give a brand new Heaven and a brand new earth. He will take away the curse of sin, remove the thorns and thistles, and give me a brand new kingdom. I am a part of that promise, but I don't have it yet. But God says it's as sure of a deal as I can make. "In fact," He is saying, "I'll give you a down payment promising you that what I started by saving your soul and writing your name in the book of Heaven, I will finish by giving you a brand new body, a brand new Heaven, a brand new earth, and no more curse. To promise you that and to make sure you know I'm keeping My Word, I'll give you My Holy Spirit inside of you!"

There are many wonderful promises waiting for the

saved person, but I am not referring to receiving the Spirit of God when you get saved. In this chapter, I am addressing the obtaining of the influence and the power of the Holy Spirit for me to help you.

The Bible gives some important instruction about the Holy Spirit in Luke 11. My burden is to try to help you do what all Christians are supposed to be doing, and that is to get the Holy Spirit's help. His help is needed not only in living the Christian life, but also in the most important work of all, and that is to help you help other Christians live the Christian life.

One word summarizes all of Christianity, and that word is *others*. The sooner you and I learn that word, the sooner we will see how much we need God's help. The sooner we obtain God's help; the sooner we become more Christlike.

In order to understand the work of the Holy Spirit, I need to explain some doctrine. Jesus' disciples are asking Him, "Where do You get Your power? When You pray, things happen. How do You get things to happen like that?"

Jesus said, "Let me break it down to two areas. First of all, I get things for Me. I take care of Myself or rather My Father does. I think what you're asking me is, 'How do I get things for Me?' or 'How do I get through the hard times?' or 'How do I handle situations like the death of Lazarus or John the Baptist?' or 'How do I handle the problems of life?' I think you're asking Me, 'How do I get from God those things that I personally need?' "

Jesus accurately read between the lines, and the disciples said, "Yes, that's what we mean. When You pray, You get things for yourself."

Jesus was saying, "Yes, when I pray to My Father, I get My bread. He cares for Me. I am not hungry. I do not have to do without. I can tell you how you can get God to take care of you, but I think you're asking a deeper question, aren't you? Aren't you asking Me how I have the influence and the power to help **other** people? Aren't you asking Me how I can heal the blind? Aren't you asking Me how I have influence over the lame, and the sick, and the deaf, and the dumb? Aren't you asking Me how I have influence to preach with hundreds getting converted? Aren't you asking Me how I fulfill the will of God for my life?"

"Sure."

The disciples were asking two things: (1) How do I get things from God for myself? and (2) How do I get God to help me help other people? The answers to both of these questions center around the Holy Spirit. The Holy Spirit is the secret or answer to both questions.

We need the Holy Spirit to help us in our daily lives. Husbands and wives need the Holy Spirit to help them have a good marriage. They are not going to have the kind of marriage that is Christ-honoring, God-honoring, Bible-honoring, and church-honoring if they do not have the Holy Spirit of God helping them in their marriage.

Moms and dads need the Holy Spirit to help them rear their children. Parents will not rear Christ-honoring, God-fearing, Bible-loving, and church-going kids if they do not have the Holy Spirit helping them. It's hard enough to rear that type of young person with all of the published books, tapes, and materials available. However, using those materials will not guarantee Christ-honoring young people; we need the help of the Holy Spirit.

The indwelling of the Holy Spirit is not just for preachers to preach a sermon. The Holy Spirit is for moms and dads to rear children. The Holy Spirit is for schoolteachers to teach in the classrooms. Teachers, you can study all you want, read all the textbooks you have, become educated and have multiple degrees listed behind your names, but you won't accomplish what God could do through you if you don't have the Holy Spirit of God helping you get it done.

I have personal needs like everyone has personal needs. I go back to that time when First Baptist Church of Hammond grieved collectively over the loss of Brother Hyles. Do you think I did not grieve the loss of my father-in-law? Do you not think it was very difficult for me when seemingly everyone talked about how well they knew Brother Hyles? In truth, many of them did not know him as well as I did. Did you think that my wife and I did not grieve? Did you think I was happy just because I was voted in as the pastor? He was my friend and my father-in-law. Of course, I grieved!

How can I grieve while I am trying to help the church members? The Holy Spirit! How do I walk onto the platform on topside and happy while the church family sits in the pews unhappy and miserable? The only way I could make it through is the only way any person is going to make it through a difficult time, and that is with the help of the Holy Spirit.

Everyone has personal needs, whether you're a husband needing help with a marriage or a wife needing help with a marriage or a mother and father needing help with child rearing or an employer needing help with employees. Whatever your needs are, you need the Holy Spirit. That is how a person survives, but that is not very much of the Christian life. In fact, getting what you need is a very small part of the Christian life.

God knows that our personal and physical needs distract us from our spiritual needs. When you get to Heaven, you're not going to get a reward for suffering with a hangnail or an ingrown toenail or going to church and still teaching your Sunday school class. Your rewards will not be based on how many personal needs you got cared for, but how much you helped other people.

Nobody is going to get a reward in Heaven because he got the most prayers answered for himself. The whole bottom line of Christianity is not what you got out of it for yourself, but what did you do for Christ?

> *Only one life, so soon will pass,*
> *Only what's done for Christ will last.*

If God says, "Yes, I answered so-and-so's prayers for himself more than anybody else's," what reward does "Mr. So-and-So" get? Like the Pharisees, he received his reward. He received all of his rewards on earth. If you got all the things you wanted from God, He probably isn't going to give you a reward for that because you got your reward—you got all you wanted. The reward is what did you do for other people?

God is saying, "I know that most of you are not as concerned for others as you should be until you have your own needs met. It's hard to pray when your stomach is growling. It's hard to care about others when you are grieving yourself." That is the why the first thing asked for in Luke 11 is, "Father, give me bread for myself" or *"Give us day by day our daily bread."*

What is He saying? He's saying, "I know you're not going to be focused on other people until I take care of your needs, so ask Me to take care of your needs. I will take care of them for you. Talk to the Father about that need. You only have to know Me on a Father/son basis for that request."

In other words, you can go to the Father, and say, "Father, I know I should live for others, and I know I should care for others, but I'm hurting. My heart is sore, my heart is pained, my mind is tired. I'm weary in body, I'm weary of flesh, I'm tempted, I'm distressed, I'm upset, I'm confused, I'm confounded, I'm in despair, and I'm kind of messed up."

God says, "Okay, I'll take care of you first." God even says you have the right to go to Him first and to ask first for your own personal needs to be met because God is saying, "I know you. You're not going to think about others until you're taken care of first." So, I only have to go to the Father to take care of me.

Then He says, "However, do you want to get down to serious business? Once that personal need is cared for, let's go to serious business. First of all, your personal, physical needs distract you from your spiritual needs. Second, your unconfessed sins will short-circuit the process. So, why don't we deal with your sins? If you are sinning, it is because you are selfish. If you're selfish, you're not going to do much of anything for anybody else."

Every moment I spend not living for others it is usually because I am living for self. Certainly I am excusing the time spent in sleeping or in taking time for personal care and hygiene and such things. Aside from the few basic needs of life, if I'm not living for others, it's because I'm focused on me.

So God says, "Okay, I'll take care of your physical needs and your personal needs because if I don't do that, you won't take care of what's really big, and that's living for others. Secondly, if you don't deal with your sin, you're not going to be living for others either because every moment not spent living for others is usually spent living for self, and that's what sin is." Sin is selfish living.

He added, "Forgive us our sins, and we'll forgive everybody else, too." It's amazing that as soon as you have your sins forgiven, you think of others. Forgive us our sins, as we forgive **others**. The word "others" comes in there. Why? Because when I stop thinking about me, I start thinking about others.

Once I've taken care of my own personal, physical needs

by my Heavenly Father, then I take care of my own sin because that is distracting my care for others; then my attention is really turned away from myself. "Friend, somebody has crossed my path, and I don't have what he needs. How am I going to help him? What I have, even though it's from You, is not sufficient to take care of them."

God says, "Now, we're down to business. I took care of your needs. You take care of your sins. Now, let's both of us take care of others."

However, the Christian has to qualify for both of these. In Luke 11, the Bible explains two relationships. The first one is, to whom do I go if I need bread? The answer, of course, is that I go to my Heavenly Father. However, if I want loaves for others, to whom do I go? My Heavenly Friend is the One to Whom I go.

As we have already established, two different names are used in Luke 11—*Father* and *Friend*. Actually, the Bible describes seven different relationships that every Christian has with God. I'm going to address those seven relationships to show how a person may first qualify to get his personal needs cared for, and secondly, how he can get loaves for somebody else.

Seven Relationships

1. **Creator and Creation.** Everybody who has been born or conceived in the womb has this relationship; however, the Bible does not say, "When you pray, say, 'Our Creator.' " The Bible says, "When you pray, say, '*Our Father.* '" The Creator God is obligated to do nothing for you. By virtue of your being created and on this earth, God owes you nothing. You owe God everything.

2. **Redeemer and Redeemed.** By the virtue of being born again, you are His redeemed; My Redeemer owes the

Christian nothing more than eternal life in Heaven. He has promised me a brand new Heaven, but I don't get that now. He promised me a brand new earth, but I don't get that now. He gave me His Holy Spirit, but I don't get advantage of that because at this point, I am not qualified to use Him fully—even though I possess Him.

Just because your daddy has a car in the garage doesn't mean you have the right to use it. It's there, but you don't get to use it even though you might possess it.

The Bible doesn't say to pray to our Redeemer. In fact, the only time Redeemer is referred to is when I'm praising God for what He's done for me.

So, if I'm only born again, then I do not get bread for myself, and I surely do not get loaves for somebody else.

3. God and People. II Corinthians 6:16 says, *"...and I will be their God, and they shall be my people."* That verse means a liberal does not have the right to pray to God because God is not his God. He's not one of God's people because he's not even redeemed. All he is is created, and the Creator owes that liberal nothing.

Nobody has a right to call God, "God," unless he is separated from the wrong crowd. The Bible does not say, "Our God." It says, *"Our Father."* God owes His people one thing, and that's a special relationship that you belong to Him and He belongs to you.

He says, "I don't owe you any favors. You're just now seeing that I redeemed you, and I made you. The light's still coming on in your head. I owe you nothing except a brand new Heaven, a brand new earth, your soul redeemed in Heaven, and a brand new body someday; but right now I owe you nothing."

"Do you mean when I pray, Brother Schaap, if I am in the wrong crowd, I can't pray?"

You can pray, but God is not obligated to answer your

prayer. God says, "I'm a merciful God. I send rain on the just and the unjust. I'm sometimes good to the wrong crowd, but that's My business. I am not obligated to help the wrong crowd, and when you run with that crowd, I'm not obligated to help you. Just because you're saved, I'm not obligated to help you, and just because you're a member of the human race, I'm surely not obligated to help you."

4. Father and Son. II Corinthians 6:17 and 18 says, *"Wherefore come out from among them* [that's the wrong crowd!], *and be ye separate, saith the Lord, and touch not the unclean thing; and I will receive you, And will be a Father unto you, and ye shall be my sons and daughters, saith the Lord Almighty."* What is this verse talking about here? When I leave the wrong crowd, God is now my God, and I'm His people. When I put away the wrong things that crowd taught me, then I become God's son or daughter.

"You're my son, and you live in my house, but it's not enough that you leave the wrong crowd. That's important, but don't you bring the wrong crowd's stuff into my house." There are two steps mentioned in these two verses. Many parents have kept their kids from running with the wrong crowd, but they keep finding the wrong crowd's junk in their children's room.

God is saying, "As long as you're bringing wrong-crowd junk into your home, then you haven't left that crowd in your heart." Until you get to the point where you say, "Not only do I not want the wrong crowd, but I also don't want any part of the smoking, drinking, lying, stealing, dancing, music, or wickedness. I want to be a separated man." Then God says, "That's my boy."

When you pray and say, "Our Father," God just became obligated. As God, He has obligated Himself to help this man, but not the other men. When God sees His child clean outside and inside, then He says, "That's my boy! You're trying to act, walk, talk, smell, and look like one of My children, and I'm proud of you!" When you reach that stage of your life, He's obligated to help you and to take care of you. That man has the right to go to God and say, "I have some personal needs."

"What do you need?"

"I need daily bread."

"How much?"

"Daily bread."

"Okay, here it is," God says.

Only when the Christian has reached this stage is he qualified to ask God for the Holy Spirit and the fruits of the Spirit. God is obligated to give a Christian these things at this stage.

5. Lord and Servant. At this stage in the Christian's life, He is not only cleaning up his life, but he is also starting to say, "Father, is there anything You want me to do? The Bible has some commands, and I'm obligated to keep those commands."

God says, "Since you feel obligated to keep My commands, then I'm obligated to care for you like a Lord does for his servant. I'll pay you some compensation for taking care of me."

This stage is where you start getting into the rewards of life. It's simple: you obey, and God rewards. You read your Bible, and God speaks to you. You go soul winning, and you see somebody saved. God doesn't care what your title is in the church; but when you obey, you will get rewarded, though you won't receive most of those rewards until Heaven. Still, at this stage you are not qualified to have the Holy Spirit work through you to minister to other people. God might choose you to get a job done, but God is still not obligated to use you.

6. Friend and Friend. John 15:14 says, *"Ye are my*

friends, if ye do whatsoever I command you." More than this verse qualifies that friendship is laying down your life sacrificially. It is obedience not compelled by the thought, "Do I get something for it?" Rather, it is obedience that says, "I love you so much. You first loved me. May I please lay my life down for you, Friend?"

"God, can I go where You're going?" "Father, would you help me do what You want done?" "I want to live now like I was living with You already in Heaven."

God responds, "That's My buddy. That's My friend. He's more concerned with what I want done than with what he wants done."

This is why it's so important how you live privately because how you live privately determines how you qualify. God says, "If I can trust you and if you behave yourself privately as though you were at church, then you're My son and thy daughter, but I'm still not going to invest My Holy Spirit power in you until you qualify as a friend."

7. Groom and Bride. Christians cannot obtain the groom and bride relationship on earth. That relationship is reached at the Rapture when we see Jesus Christ face to face. All of the others are all available to the Christian while on earth.

Christian, have you seen yourself in one of these relationships? Qualifying for the Spirit, the crux of the Christian life, is living for others. Since God knows I'm not going to live for others until my own personal needs are cared for, He says, "Okay, you qualify, and I'll obligate. You make Me your Father, and you become My child. I'll make myself obligated to fill your needs so you will not be selfish. You will not get a reward in Heaven for having your needs met. You get rewards in Heaven for living for others. Do you want to live for others? You have to have a friend."

In the story of Luke 11, God says, "Even though you're

My friend, I'm not going to give you what you want." The friend is the only one who's allowed to nag God.

God says, "I'm a busy God, and I'm a very careful investor." You can get personal things you want from God if you qualify as a Father/son, but before you buy the business, and God invests thousands and His Holy Spirit's power in you God says, "Let's check your spiritual bankbook. Let's check your tithing record. Let's check how you care for your spouse. Let's see how you treat your family members. I want to see if you really are My friend."

"Yes, God, I am Your friend."

"You're right. What do you want?"

"God, I want You to invest in me."

"Prove it."

"Okay, here's my record. Here's the right I have to come to You, God. I have gladly and willingly sacrificed my life for You. I have tithed. I've obeyed. I read your Word. I'm on my knees. You can invest in me."

God says, "The only person who can talk to Me that way is someone who is surrendered."

Bus captain, have you earned the right to address God as Friend? Sunday school teacher, have you earned the right to address God as a Friend? Christian school teacher, have you earned the right to address God as Friend?

God says, "Nobody has the right to ask Me for that kind of investment unless he has qualified himself, and the qualification is to be a friend with God."

Have you ever wondered why Brother Hyles had such incredible power? Isn't it amazing how he always had what it seemed he needed? How many times did he come to you, and say, "I need help"? How much money did he borrow from you? His resources weren't out of the world; yet, he always seemed to have what he needed. Why? He had the Father/son relationship with God. More than that, why is it

[164]

he always had what you needed? Why is it that when you went to his office he always seemed to have what you needed? Why? He was a friend of God. As a friend of God, he had the right to go to God and say, "God, I need You now."

When God said, "Prove it," Brother Hyles would take out a list and say, "There's nothing on the list for me. There's a whole lot of things for other people I'm praying for. I'm going to get it." Hundreds of us were recipients of his friendship relationship with God. Why? One man got loaves from a God Who was his buddy.

Did you ever wonder why Abraham never wanted for anything? He was a friend of God. Why did he get the blessings? Why did he get to be the father of the nation of Israel? Why did he get to be the one who acted out salvation with his son Isaac? Why is there more written about him? He was the one who went to God and said, "God, it's not like You to judge the righteous and the unrighteous." Before you talk to God like that, you better qualify! God says, "You're right. What else do you want?"

Wouldn't you love to live a life where you can go to God and say, "God, You know I qualify. You know I have a right to it. I've earned it. I'm qualified. You're my Buddy. You're my Pal. You're my Friend. What are you going to do about it, God?"

God is going to say, "I'm going to give you what you need." Wouldn't you love to have that relationship? Then qualify!

CHAPTER NINE

The Great Spiritual Secret

■ ■ ■

Isaiah 44:1-8 says, *"Yet now hear, O Jacob my servant; and Israel, whom I have chosen: Thus saith the LORD that made thee, and formed thee from the womb, which will help thee; Fear not, O Jacob, my servant; and thou, Jesurun, whom I have chosen. For I will pour water upon him that is thirsty, and floods upon the dry ground: I will pour my spirit upon thy seed, and my blessing upon thine offspring: And they shall spring up as among the grass, as willows by the water courses. One shall say, I am the LORD's; and another shall call himself by the name of Jacob; and another shall subscribe with his hand unto the LORD, and surname himself by the name of Israel. Thus saith the LORD the King of Israel, and his redeemer the LORD of hosts; I am the first, and I am the last; and beside me there is no God. And who, as I, shall call, and shall declare it, and set it in order for me, since I appointed the ancient people? and the things that are coming, and shall come, let them shew unto them. Fear ye not, neither be afraid: have not I told thee from that time, and have declared it? ye are even my witnesses. Is there a God beside me? yea, there is no God; I know not any."*

Christian schools are one of the easiest places in which to backslide. To be sure, the Christian school offers a far better education and fewer opportunities for sinful activities.

As far as a young person's spirit growing strong and his becoming a strong spiritual Christian, he is at times more at risk of not growing in a Christian school. Why? There are several reasons.

A friend of mine once said, "Brother Schaap, you preach to a lot of teenagers. Warn them not to lower their guard while they attend a Christian school."

I asked, "What do you mean?"

"I went to a public school for the first eight or nine grades," he said. "My dad had left our house, and my mother had to work several jobs to make ends meet, but finally she saved enough money to put me in a Christian school. She had often warned me while I was attending the public school, 'Don't listen to those fellows who smoke and look at dirty magazines.' I went to the public school with my guard up. Mama had pumped so much fear and warning into me that I was afraid to do anything wrong, and I didn't do anything foolish. Though I wasn't a great Christian, I had a pretty good testimony.

"The first morning I left to go to the Christian school, Mom was so happy she cried tears of joy and gladness. When it came time for my first recess in a Christian school, the boys got a hold of me, and I learned how to smoke. One week later during recess, I learned how to drink. One month later during recess, I learned how to fornicate.

"I'm sorry to say that I learned about pornography, fornication, and everything wicked that Mama had guarded me from at the public school. My classmates at the Christian school introduced me to it all. They were worse than the public school kids, but they had on all the Christian school garb. I fell victim to them immediately, and I am still messed up today in my thinking."

I don't worry about that kind of a situation happening in our Christian school. We have excellent leadership, and that will not take place in our Christian school system. What I do worry about is the young person attending Hyles-Anderson College or City Baptist Schools or Hammond Baptist Schools letting that Christian school environment substitute for their internal, personal passion for God.

If an individual does not have that internal passion for God, all the good circumstances and all the best environment in the world cannot affect him positively. In fact, those good circumstances and that best environment usually affect a young person negatively. I particularly want to address young people in this chapter. I want to share the great spiritual secret about being filled with the Holy Spirit and the work of the Holy Spirit in your life.

Teenagers, what kind of school year do you want? Young people in college, what kind of college life do you want? Do you want to experience the same old year as the previous year? Did you receive lots of demerits, get into lots of trouble, experience a boring, backslidden year, and endure one more year of low productivity? You didn't do much and nothing much happened; you received average grades, and you were more concerned about dating than walking with God. You spent the year being preoccupied with peripheral things. What kind of year do you want?

The secret to everything God has is wanting it. There are no magical secrets; it's how bad do you want it? Isaiah 44:3 says, *"For I will pour water upon him that is thirsty, and floods upon the dry ground...."* James 4:2 says, *"...ye have not, because ye ask not."*

The number one reason for unanswered prayers is that you do not pray. People come to me and say, "I don't get things from God." The answer to that situation is easy—you don't ask.

"Oh, I ask," you declare.

You don't ask. You tiptoe around. You dodge the real issue. You write a little petition and wave it toward God and say, "I need something. I need something." When you don't get it, you say, "Prayer doesn't work for me." You have no idea what prayer is all about because you have never learned to ask and to plead.

God promises, *"For I will pour water upon him that is thirsty, and floods upon the dry ground...,"* and He also contends, *"...ye have not, because ye ask not."*

Isaiah 41:17 and 18 say, *"When the poor and needy seek water, and there is none, and their tongue faileth for thirst, I the LORD will hear them, I the God of Israel will not forsake them. I will open rivers in high places, and fountains in the midst of the valleys: I will make the wilderness a pool of water, and the dry land springs of water."* God is saying, "If you're dry or thirsty, I have what you need. How badly do you want it?"

If God is so willing to pour out His Spirit upon His children like a flood upon a dry ground, then the only logical answer for those who do not have it is they don't want it badly enough to get it! The answer to everything God has is, "Do you want it badly enough to get it?"

I am amazed at people who come to my office and say, "I'm having a hard time financially, Brother Schaap. I'm just not making ends meet."

Generally I ask, "Where do you work?"

"For three months I've tried to get a job."

Don't give me that excuse! Get a job! The person who does not have a job spends as much time looking for a job as he wants to work. If you want a 40-hour a week job, then spend 40 hours looking for a job. What some would rather do is trot to my office and call that looking for a job. My office is not a job placement office, although I love to help people. I have some phone numbers of companies who call me and say, "Pastor, if you have people who want to work, send them to us. We'll hire them."

Unfortunately, I hear too many comments like, "Well, I tried that job before, but I don't like that kind of work." I ask again, "How badly do you want it?"

God says, *"For I will pour water upon him that is thirsty, and floods upon the dry ground,..."* and *"...ye have not, because ye ask not."*

The excuse comes, "I tried that praying business, and it doesn't work." You pray as many hours as you need the answers. You pray and pray and pray and pray and fast and plead and pray, and you will get the answer. God is no respecter of persons!

I was talking to a pastor several years ago, and he said, "Brother Schaap, we're building a big building."

I asked, "What's it going to cost you?"

He said, "It's going to cost us a million dollars, but I have my money. Let me tell you how I got it. I was reading my Bible, and it occurred to me when I read the verse, *"God is no respecter of persons,"* that that was the greatest prayer promise in the whole Bible."

I agreed, "It surely is."

He continued, "I went to God and said, 'Okay, God of D.L. Moody, Jack Hyles, Lee Roberson, Charles Spurgeon, J. Frank Norris, W. B. Riley, and those great leaders that I have heard about getting big answers of prayer from you. I'm a little old nobody, but You're not a respecter of persons, so You better come through!' God did! The next afternoon I got a call, and someone gave me a check for nearly a half million dollars.

I'm not saying every person who prays is going to get a half million dollars, but I am saying that God is no respecter of persons. If you want it badly enough, God has obligated Himself to give you what He has promised and made available to you. The answer is, God says, *"For I will pour water*

[171]

upon him that is thirsty, and floods upon the dry ground..." and "*...ye have not, because ye ask not.*"

God asks, "How badly do you want it?"

How badly do you want to be filled with the Holy Spirit? How badly do you want the power of God? How badly do you want the mighty baptism of the Spirit of God? God says, "*I will pour water upon him that is thirsty.*" The great spiritual secret is wanting it.

Matthew 7:7 and 8 say, "*Ask, and it shall be given you; seek, and ye shall find; knock, and it shall be opened unto you. For every one that asketh receiveth; and he that seeketh findeth; and to him that knocketh it shall be opened.*" Verse 11 continues, "*If ye then, being evil, know how to give good gifts unto your children, how much more shall your Father which is in heaven give good things to them that ask him?*" Luke 11:13 states, "*...how much more shall your heavenly Father give the Holy Spirit to them that ask Him?*" God says, "*For I will pour water upon him that is thirsty, and floods upon the dry ground...*" and "*...ye have not, because ye ask not.*" The great secret is, "Do you want it?"

Some live on dry ground. The prophet Ezekiel said he was standing by the temple and looked down, and water began to flow underneath the threshold of the door. As he watched for a while, the water flowed higher and higher. Ezekiel called for a man, and he measured it. The man walked out a thousand measuring sticks, and it was ankle deep. When Ezekiel told him to measure it again, he said, "I walked out a thousand more, and it was up to my waist." Ezekiel told him to measure it yet again, and he said, "I walked out more, and it was so deep I had to swim in it."

Some Christians are standing on dry ground. Others are standing in ankle deep water; some are standing in water up to their waist. Others are swimming and almost drowning in the blessings of God! Why? Those Christians found the answer, "*For I will pour water upon him that is thirsty, and floods*

THE GREAT SPIRITUAL SECRET

upon the dry ground..." and "*...ye have not, because ye ask not.*"
God said, "I'm not a respecter of persons, so who wants it?"

If God is so eager to give His power to us, and we do not
have it, what's the problem? I believe we do not want it
because we are filled with something else. We talk about
being filled. We read about being filled with the Holy Spirit.
We attend church and hear about the filling of the Holy
Spirit. We may walk an aisle, and say, "God I really, really
want Your power," but how much time do we spend pleading and begging for the mighty baptism of the Spirit of
God?

God baptized Brother Hyles, and He's no respecter of
persons. He baptized Moses, and He's no respecter of persons. Every child of God has a right to go to Him and say,
"God of Moses and Joshua, You baptized them with the
Spirit of God! God of John the Baptist, You baptized him
from the womb with the Spirit of God. God, I read in Your
Word that You are not a respecter of persons. It's little, old,
nobody me, and I'm calling in. You said, 'I have not because
I ask not;' well, I'm asking!"

God answers, "*For I will pour water upon him that is thirsty,
and floods upon the dry ground;...*" and "*...ye have not, because ye
ask not.*"

I have to assume that if the power of the Holy Spirit is
so available and you don't have it, it's because you don't
want it. Wanting it is the secret to everything.

If I lost my job tonight, I promise you, I would have a
job tomorrow! You ask, "How would you do it?" I would
have a job because I want one!

Some ask, "How can I make it financially?" Figure out
how, want it, and go get it. That is exactly what I did!

You say, "I don't have all of the opportunities." May I
testify? I came to the Calumet area, knowing not one person, having no leads or connections. I came to this area

[173]

dumb and poor, but the difference was, I just wanted it. I wasn't connected because I got married; I didn't get married for several years after moving to the Calumet region.

You say, "Well, I've been here for 12 years, and I haven't yet graduated." I say, you don't want that diploma badly enough.

Everything that God has comes to those who desire it. Proverbs 18:1 says, *"Through desire a man, having separated himself, seeketh and intermeddleth with all wisdom."* How badly do you want it?

God questions, "Is anyone thirsty? I have water. I'll pour water upon the dry ground."

"Well, maybe tomorrow," He hears. Or, He hears, "Maybe during the Fall Program," or "Maybe during the Spring Program," or "Not now, maybe later."

The bottom line is, God is so eager to baptize you with the Spirit. He is so eager to pour out His Spirit upon you. God is so eager to use you. It does not matter who you are! Whether you are a public school student, a mission man, a homeless man, a deaf or blind person, a healthy person, God wants to use you. God says, *"For I will pour water upon him that is thirsty, and floods upon the dry ground..."* and *"...ye have not, because ye ask not."* How badly do you want it?

The bottom line is desire. How badly do you want His Spirit? We're filled with all kinds of things that keep us from really wanting it.

God says to the prophet Jeremiah in Jeremiah 5:7-9, *"How shall I pardon thee for this? thy children have forsaken me, and sworn by them that are no gods: when I had fed them to the full, they then committed adultery, and assembled themselves by troops in the harlots' houses. They were as fed horses in the morning: every one neighed after his neighbour's wife. Shall I not visit for these things?..."* God is saying, "I wanted to bless you, and I gave you good things. When you were full of those things,

[174]

you turned away from Me and to other things. Now you're so full of those other things, you don't want Me anymore." The reason why some do not want what God has for them is because they have desired other things and have become satisfied with those other things. What do I mean by that statement? When I have all I could possibly need or want, I am most tempted to sin against my provider.

Children who have everything they could want are generally the ones who sin most against their parents. When you get everything you could want, and when you get your way, you sin.

Parents, don't let a 15- or 16-year-old kid tell you how it will be. Of course, you should listen, act as a sounding board, and give the young person a careful hearing. Don't be afraid to say, "Tell me all about it. I want to hear every thought you have." After you have listened then say, "Thank you very much for explaining and sharing with me. Let's pray about it. I sympathize with you. God bless you, now here's how we will deal with that situation."

Too many adults let their teenagers run the home. The young people even tell me they control the home. You ask, "What am I supposed to do?" Try using a big board across the posterior. You say, "Did you do that?" Yes! Too many parents are scared of their own kids. They are afraid their teen might run away.

My son said one day, "Dad, if I ever rebelled or did anything stupid, you wouldn't let me run away would you?"

I said, "No, that's not an option." I added with an evil smirk, "I'd kill you before you'd walk out on me."

He said, "That's what I thought."

My son knew he wasn't going to run away from me, and I am not going to kick him out of the house. Of course, he knew I was only exaggerating my point when I said I'd kill him. I will not say, "If you don't obey me, I'm going to kick you out of the house." They'll be selling Popsicles in Hell before I let my 16-year-old son tell me how it's going to be. I love my son, and he loves me; but he isn't going to tell me how it's going to be! Neither should your teenager be allowed to tell you how it's going to be.

What happens is too many parents let their teenagers get filled so full. We let them have anything they want. They run the roost and rule the house; by doing so, they themselves turn against their very provider.

As a Christian, when I'm full from God's blessings, so often I find myself getting upset with the very God Who blessed me! When you give a person all he asks for, you create an unsatisfied person. The more a person receives, the more he wants. The greater his appetites, the more perverted he becomes in satisfying those appetites.

Some people have craved and craved the wrong things until their appetites were filled. Now, their only satisfaction is perversion and distortion until their minds are gutters and their souls are like sewers filled constantly with the world, Hollywood, and Hell. Why? They got full of the things they thought they had to have one day, and they stopped begging and pleading for the things God had for them.

Proverbs 27:7 says, *"The full soul loatheth an honeycomb; but to the hungry soul every bitter thing is sweet."* When a person gets hungry enough or thirsty enough for something, he will go to God and beg and plead, "God, I want it."

My family used to visit the home of Mrs. Louise Clifton, who is now in Heaven. I don't believe my wife will mind my saying that Mrs. Clifton probably prepared the best food I have ever tasted in my life. Mrs. Clifton was an outstanding cook. When we went to her house, I would eat until I got sick.

She made the best pork roast you'd ever want to eat.

With the pork roast, she would prepare mashed potatoes, sweet potato pie, and homemade hot muffins with fresh strawberry or raspberry preserves. While I was eating, Mrs. Clifton would look at me and say, "You're getting uncomfortable, aren't you?"

I would just say, "Keep bringing it!"

The meal time was usually about an hour or so. After everyone else had stopped eating, I would continue to eat and eat and eat and eat. When I could not hold anymore, I would undo my belt buckle. When that didn't help, I undid the fastener. When I was almost miserable, she would ask, "Do you have room for dessert?"

My standard answer was, "No, but bring it on anyway."

On more than one occasion, I would lie on the floor and undo all the harnesses I could on my britches because there was no room to breathe. She would give me a towel or a blanket to put over me. I would lie on the floor literally panting.

She would look at me and say, "You're miserable."

"Yeah," I agreed, "but it's a good misery." I call that being full!

When we waddled out of her house to go home, nothing sounded good. I felt like I would be full enough for the next three months. When you get that full, nothing sounds good—not your favorite dessert or your favorite cracker or your favorite cookie or your favorite candy—nothing sounds good. Why? You're so full! *The full soul loatheth an honeycomb; but to the hungry soul every bitter thing is sweet.*

The great secret to everything God has is wanting it or desiring it. Jeremiah said He gave some things, but people took the things He gave and perverted them. They got so full of them that their appetites were distorted; all they developed was one big appetite for all of the wrong things. Why is that? When I have all that I could possibly need or want, then is when I find I am most tempted to sin against my provider. Why is that? When a person is given all that he asks for, an unsatisfied person is the result. Why is that? The more things a person receives, the more he wants; and the greater his appetites, the more perverted he becomes in satisfying those appetites.

These people in Ezekiel's day were not fed worldly things; they were fed by God. They were full of good things.

When our schools open in August, it is amazing to me how we actually have students who are begging and pleading and willing to get up at three or four o'clock in the morning to catch a bus they will have to ride anywhere from one to four hours to go to City Baptist Schools. On the other hand, we have some students at Hammond Baptist saying, "I ain't going to that school this year." *"The full soul loatheth an honeycomb; but to the hungry soul every bitter thing is sweet."*

God says, "I've filled you, and now you don't even want what I provide."

When I think about how my father-in-law literally gave his heart, his blood, his sweat, his energy, his time away from family, and his life to build those schools and to keep them open, and you say, "I don't want to go there," it ticks me off. You don't want to go there? Are you on drugs? What's wrong with you? I love you too much not to tell you like it is, and you need your pastor sometimes to tell you where you stand.

God says, "I've filled you, and now you don't even want what I provide."

While I was a young college student still at my home church in Holland, Michigan, I dated a girl with whom I thought about getting serious. One day, just the two of us went soul winning together. We even brought our converts to church on a Wednesday night. That same evening, the pastor stood up to speak and introduced his sermon with, "I'm going to change my sermon tonight. I want to talk about the sin of parents who let good godly young men and godly young ladies go out soul winning together as a date." He could not have gotten any more blunt. There were only two young people dating in the entire church! That night, probably less than 50 people were at the service, and there were only two dating teenagers—she and I!

I sat on the third row with our converts, and the pastor spent 45 minutes reaming me out because I was a good godly kid who was going to throw away my testimony. He also said I was going to ruin everything God had for me because I wasn't smart enough to know how to date. I sat there as he pointed his finger at me and yelled at me. What did I do? I walked the aisle, got right with God, and promised never to date unchaperoned again.

"The full soul loatheth an honeycomb; but to the hungry soul every bitter thing is sweet." There's some things you should want and some things you should not want; you're filled with the wrong things, and that's why God's Spirit is not working through you. That's why you don't see things God's way. Young people, I love you too much to allow you to bring that kind of attitude to our schools. *"I will pour water upon him that is thirsty."* Why don't you have that right attitude?

1. Gratitude must equal goodness. When God brings goodness toward me, I have to equal that goodness with gratitude. If my gratitude does not equal His goodness, His goodness can quickly exceed my appreciation, and I begin to start thinking I deserve all of this goodness. I become overwhelmed and smothered with the goodness of God, and before you know it, I'm so full of the goodness of God, I have no room for anything else. I am panting.

Some of you have been spoiled by a good Christian

[179]

school. When gratitude does not match goodness, one becomes suffocated with the goodness of God. Then, he doesn't want the things of God, and he desires perverted appetites. That's where sin gains entrance.

You see, for everything good God does for you, you have to have equal gratitude to match that goodness. God's goodness is greater than my gratitude, and if I don't find gratitude equal to that goodness, that goodness will overwhelm me, smother me, and push me right down where I eventually want nothing but perverted appetites.

A perverted appetite is nothing more than a proper appetite that did not express itself in gratitude. You don't find the perverted appetite. It is a good thing that has become distorted, perverted, twisted, demented, and out of joint. That perverted appetite comes when I don't have gratitude that matches goodness.

So, the secret is to find gratitude. When my gratitude matches the goodness of God, it provides me a greater appetite for the right things of God. The goodness of God must be matched by gratitude.

2. **Forgiveness must match failure.** Perhaps someone wounds my spirit. "I can't believe you did that! My faith in humanity is shaken!" Yes, your faith is shaken because you did not have enough forgiveness to match another's foolishness, and that sin rolled right over you. You cannot deal with the fact that someone is as human as you are.

So, the failure of somebody overwhelms me until I'm panting, and I have no room for anything else. Why am I not filled with the Spirit of God? I'm filled with anger and bitterness about somebody else's failures. If my forgiveness does not match their failures, then I'm filled with pity, anger, bitterness, and I have no room for the Spirit of God to work in me.

People—teachers, principals, pastors, administrators,

staff, parents, and friends—will fail you. The secret is to match the failures with forgiveness.

3. Personal holiness must exceed worldly temptation. The world comes at you, pushing you down. The world's styles, its music, its system, its depressing way of living discourages you. You must match the world's temptations with personal holiness and push it back. If you don't have enough personal holiness, then you need some help. One person's holiness may be no match for the world, and that is exactly why he needs the teachers, preachers, the Sunday school class, the bus route, this church, the school principals. Why? Their personal holiness can help him push back the world.

The world often gains a hold and pushes you down, and what happens then is you have no room for anything else. You are so filled with the world that you don't want the things of God. There is not a teenager who is strong enough to handle the onslaught of the world. That is why he needs the borrowed holiness of others.

4. Love for others must exceed love for self. That selfish person says, "I'm having a pity party. I want to listen to my kind of music, and Mom and Dad won't let me. I want to have parties, and they won't let me. I want an 11:30 p.m. curfew, and they won't let me. I've got a bad life."

You've got a King James Bible sitting on your nightstand that you don't read. You have a pastor and staff who love you. You have parents who take you to church and who paid to put you in a Christian school. You have bus captains and Sunday school teachers who love you and make sure you are in church every week. What are you crying about?

Your self has to be swallowed up or resisted by helping others. If you don't have what it takes to live for others, ask for help from your pastor, teachers, or others, and you can overcome being filled with self by living for others.

[181]

5. Confession of sin must equal committing of sin.
I hear confessions like, "Brother Schaap, I've got a bad habit of smoking cigarettes. The Devil gets me down. I'm so weak, and I have no resistance. I'm a sinner with bad habits, and I don't think God forgives me."

Two words: "Shut up!" One word: "Altar." When that person's confession matches the sinning, then he begins making room for the things of God in his life.

It would do a whole lot of good for some to stop hiding behind, "I'm a sinner." You were conceived in iniquity and born in sin. You are a sinner by birth! In other words, you are going to sin until the Rapture or until you die. I am made out of the same cloth as you are. The difference between us is simple: every time I sin, I confess.

You say, "But I have a hard time doing it." If that's true, then ask for help. Allow your pastor and teachers to remind you of your sins.

The secret to everything God has is wanting it. The problem is you don't want it badly enough. Why? If you wanted it badly enough, then when good things come from God, you'd say, "God, thank You." And if you really wanted more room, you would keep thanking Him for every good thing.

Charles Finney said, "When God uses me, I spend three times more time thanking God than I did asking for His blessing." When I read that, it opened up a whole world to me. My gratitude must exceed my perception of God's goodness.

No one could ever out-gratitude God's goodness, but if we start thanking God for everything in our lives, it will be amazing how much room we would have for God's power and Spirit. We don't have it because we don't want it badly enough. If we wanted it, we would match God's goodness with gratitude. If we wanted it badly enough, then we would match the failures of others with forgiveness. We would match the worldly pressure with personal holiness. We would match love of self with living for others. We would match the sin with confession.

In other words, by making room in your life, you provide an appetite for the things of God by gratitude, by forgiveness, by personal holiness, by love and living for others, and by confessing sin. Anyone can make room for the Spirit of God, but he must want it.

CHAPTER TEN

What I Really Want from the Spirit

▪ ▪ ▪

Acts 1:3-8 says, *"To whom also he shewed himself alive after his passion by many infallible proofs, being seen of them forty days, and speaking of the things pertaining to the kingdom of God: And, being assembled together with them, commanded them that they should not depart from Jerusalem, but wait for the promise of the Father, which, saith he, ye have heard of me. For John truly baptized with water; but ye shall be baptized with the Holy Ghost not many days hence. When they therefore were come together, they asked of him, saying, Lord, wilt thou at this time restore again the kingdom to Israel? And he said unto them, It is not for you to know the times or the seasons, which the Father hath put in his own power. But ye shall receive power, after that the Holy Ghost is come upon you: and ye shall be witnesses unto me both in Jerusalem, and in all Judæa, and in Samaria, and unto the uttermost part of the earth."*

In this passage, there is what I call a little play on words. In order to understand it, you would have to study it very carefully in the English and know some Greek. As a rule, I don't think we ever have to know any Greek or Hebrew to understand the truths of the Bible. Still, God does raise up preachers to help His people understand the Word of God. By profession, the preacher should do a little more in-depth study.

In verse seven, Jesus is speaking to His disciples. He says, *"It is not for you to know the times or the seasons, which the Father hath put in his own power."* That word, *power,* is the Greek word *exousia* which means "delegated authority" or "appointed authority." The word is used like the men on the First Baptist Church staff. They were delegated by Brother Hyles when he hired them or by someone else to hold their position. They have some authority because they were hired or because of a position they hold.

A father has delegated or appointed authority. A mother also has delegated authority in that home. A pastor has delegated authority in a church. As pastor of First Baptist Church of Hammond, I have delegated or appointed authority. When I was voted in on March 7, 2001, I was appointed authority in this church. I have *exousia* power. Every superintendent, principal, or schoolteacher has *exousia* power or appointed authority or delegated authority.

Verse eight continues, *"But ye shall receive power...."* This is the play on words. This use of the word *power* is not the same power used in verse seven. This word *power* is *dunamis* which is the same word as "dynamite" or "dynamic." It means the power of influence.

The first *power* is authority or appointed authority or delegated authority, much like voting in the mayor of a city. The disciples craved power—*exousia* power; they desired a title or position. Likewise, many people today crave *exousia* power. That desire does not always come across to others as haughtiness or arrogance. It is not wrong to want power. In the eyes of many people, I have, as the pastor of First Baptist Church of Hammond, the premier *exousia* power.

What I want, however, is *dunamis* power. Exactly what is *dunamis*? That is the influence a person has within the realm of *exousia*. For instance, Hammond's Mayor Dedelow has *exousia*, or appointed authority. Does he then have *dunamis* or influence? I do not know, but we will find out on election day.

Dunamis is the power of influence that Dad has in the position of *exousia* father. *Dunamis* is the influence that a mother, which is a position of *exousia* power, has within the confines of *exousia*. *Dunamis* is the power a Sunday school teacher has as *exousia*, having been appointed as a teacher.

How much *exousia* do you have? I don't want to worry about *exousia*. I want to worry about *dunamis*. If I worry about *dunamis*, the *exousia* will take care of itself.

Too many people crave *exousia*, who haven't done the *dunamis* to deserve the *exousia*. They have not had the influence to earn the right to have the position.

I want to address what I really want from the Spirit. I cannot know what others want from the Spirit. However, when I do marriage counseling, I'm afraid that what some want is the wrong thing. When I counsel with your families, I'm afraid that what many want is the wrong thing. Many want the Holy Spirit to be leverage by right of occupation or position to control people and to force them into subjection and obedience. The sad thing is that many of these people have never earned the *dunamis* to operate within the confines of the *exousia*.

What am I saying? I'm saying I want to influence others more than I want a position. I want to earn the right more than to hold the position. It is far more important to me that standing behind this sacred pulpit is a man who has been elected to hold the position that any intelligent-thinking younger pastor would have trembled to think about in his private moments. It does not matter to me nearly as much that you voted me in, as do I have something credible to offer you. First Baptist Church of Hammond, Indiana, had many choices who could have been voted in as pastor. My fear was not that the pulpit committee would not be able to come up with names. My fear was would the man who stands in this pulpit have earned the right to stand in this pulpit.

I do not know if I earned the right. You put that vote of approval on me, but what happens in my heart—what I really want from the Spirit is to know that when I stand behind this pulpit that I've earned the right with God to do so. Earning that right is far more important to me than having a position or having my name on the letterhead as pastor or having my picture on the brochures, tracts, and bulletins. What is far more important to me is *dunamis*. What I really want from the Spirit is not *exousia*. I want the power of God to exercise within the confines of my delegated authority.

I want to be trusted more than admired. Ten thousands times more than I would have anyone say, "Would you sign my Bible?" I would far rather hear someone say, "Would you anoint me with oil?" or "Here's a prayer request; will you pray for me? I believe in your prayers." Ten thousand times more than any kind of position, I'd far rather have the trust than the admiration of the people within the confines of my *exousia*.

People seek admiration, but admiration is a by-product of those who earned the right of trust. I want to help more than I want to be honored. I would rather fix a need and have nobody find out about it than to get glory for something that anyone could have done.

The Bible says the servant is the greatest. Does that mean every servant is promoted? No, it means that truly great people know that all honor is temporal. The bottom line is the greater you are, the less you seek the promotion and the less you seek the limelight. The greater you are the more you want to fix a need.

Brother Hyles taught us that every sermon should be like a greasy wrench. He said not to worry about how pretty the sermon was outlined or if it was homiletically perfect; he taught to worry about fixing a problem. He said to find something loose and tighten it up or find something broken and fix it. I never forgot that illustration because it made a whole lot of sense.

I want to influence others more than I want a position. I want to earn the right more than hold the position. I want to be trusted more than admired. I want to help more than be honored. I want to love more than be loved.

When a troubled married couple walks into my office and sits down across from me at a table, my heart bleeds for them because their entire marriage conflict could be solved by utilizing this principle. The husband says, "Brother Schaap, my wife doesn't understand that I'm the husband in the home." On the contrary, I think she does. She knows he is the man, and she recognizes that her husband has *exousia*. She just doesn't recognize his *dunamis*. Every problem in that marriage could be solved if he would stop worrying about his *exousia*, and start worrying about his *dunamis*. If that husband would worry about his *dunamis* and have some credibility and trustworthiness, his marriage could be healed.

Your wife's not impressed because of your title of husband. The marriage vows dim quickly. The fact that you have provided means nothing. She wants to feel the energy of *dunamis*. Your wife is not crying out because she doesn't understand that you hold the high, lofty position of husband; she's crying out because she feels you have not earned the right to hold that position. She wants your *dunamis*. She wants that spiritual energy that says, "I'm more interested in earning the right to be called your husband than to hold the position."

I got to know a married student who attended Hyles-Anderson College the same time as I did. One day he shared with me how he had his wife and five kids sit on the couch. He walked up and down in front of the couch making statements like, "I wear the pants in this family!" After I heard his story, I said to him later, "You may be wearing them, but somebody else owns them. When you have to remind your family that you wear the pants in the family, you don't." When a husband has to say to his wife, "I'm in charge here," he's not. When a pastor feels he must announce to his congregation, "Bless God, I'm the pastor, and you'll do what I say," they won't.

When a married couple commented to me, "We're so busy that we don't have time for each other," I said, "There are a thousand things you can do to convince someone you love them when you're not with them."

He said, "Well, like what?"

I said, "Leave the house in the morning, stop halfway to work, pick up the phone, call and say, 'Thinking about you; can't get my mind off you; I love you.'"

He said, "I never thought of that."

To the wife I said, "Leave a little note in his sock drawer just saying, 'I wish I was with you right now,' and add some things PG-13 rated."

You won't earn leadership until you first learn followship. You're not going to earn *exousia* until you learn *dunamis*. You're not going to earn position until you learn serving. You're not going to earn admiration and honor until you learn loving and giving and sacrificing and credibility and earning the right to give it. It's not *exousia* power you need; it's *dunamis* power you need!

For months and months, my heart's cry for First Baptist

Church of Hammond has been one continuous prayer, "Oh God, love them through me. They were loved by the best. They were cared for by the best."

Exousia doesn't help grieving people, but *dunamis* does. People aren't helped because I'm the pastor. It's the energy of love. It's the caring of love. They don't say, "Brother Schaap can help us; he signs Bibles. Brother Schaap can help us; he travels and preaches. Brother Schaap can help us; he's got a title. His name is on the stationery. I feel so comforted." No, sir! My position does not encourage them; my influence, my wisdom, my love does.

These same types of illustrations can apply to you, Dad, and that is why your teenage boy is not reaching out to you because you're trying to hide behind *exousia*. A 16-year-old boy is not very impressed by *exousia*. The title, "father," is not very impressive to a boy whose dad is hiding behind his title instead of *dunamis*. He wants the energy, passion, and feeling of his father's love. He wants to know that dad loves him. Certainly, too many parents are trying to exercise their *exousia*. They are trying to say, "I'm in charge." When people have to be reminded that you are in charge, you're not. Dad, instead of saying in your home, "I'm in charge here," ask yourself instead, "Does my daughter or son know they're loved? Do they know I care? Do they know I think about them?"

Many single people are bound up with getting a title of *exousia*. May I ask you to concentrate more on the *dunamis* energy? You single girls who say, "Is Mr. Right ever going to come around?" I say, be more concerned about *dunamis*, or earning the right, rather than earning the position.

I plead with staff members and schoolteachers who have been given *exousia*. Please don't walk around with a pompous attitude that says, "I'm Miss So-and-So or I'm Mr. So-and-So, and you have to call me by my title." Did you earn the right to hold it? Before you walk into a classroom, say, "What I want to do is prove to my students that I have earned the right to be their teacher." It's the old cliché, "People don't care about how much you know until they know how much you care."

"Brother Schaap, how does one know if he's not earned the right?" You walk around with a demerit pad giving out demerits like candy; you look for ways to throw around your weight; you look for ways to catch people doing wrong; you look for ways to say to another individual, "I'm in charge here, and you're not!" You look for ways to try to find something wrong, to be suspicious, or to be skeptical. When you are more interested in the title you will be given than the people you get to serve, that's how you can begin to know you are more interested in authority than influence.

I am not interested in a person's title; I am interested in whether or not you have earned the right to receive the honor. Have you earned the right to love and give? Do you have *dunamis*? Are you filled with the Spirit? Too many are so busy trying to change titles that they miss the opportunity to change lives.

We have a very diverse culture in First Baptist Church, and I do not know the destination of each member. I do not know God's answers for all of their lives. I have decided if a person walks in the doors of our church, it's not so important that I know that person's destination or how to get him there. The important thing is that while he is here, he knows that some church people and a pastor made him feel loved.

Sailors from Great Lakes Naval Base attend services at First Baptist Church. Many times the sailors only attend a few short weeks or months, and then they are transferred. We ask them to come forward to say goodbye to the church. When a sailor who was leaving said goodbye to the church one morning, I asked, "How long have you been attending here?"

He said, "This is my first week and my last week."

That young man attended First Baptist Church one week and heard one sermon from me. He's gone already, and I do not even know his name. Do I know his destination? No! I do know one thing, for as long as he lives he can say, "I went to First Baptist Church of Hammond one time, and I felt cared for and loved. I felt *dunamis*. I felt somebody had the power of God on his life. The people there weren't worried about position. I wasn't a feather in anyone's cap. I wasn't a notch on someone's gun. I was someone who felt the love of God through some human being."

A husband came to me and said, "Brother Schaap, give me five or six things real quick to fix my marriage."

I answered, "I don't have five or six real quick things to fix your marriage."

He countered, "You know. You've written books on it. I'd just take two or three."

I said, "You don't fix your marriage in two or three quick things. Marriage isn't a microwave popcorn machine. It doesn't work that way." (When my wife talks about men and women, she says, "Men are microwaves, and women are crock pots.") "Do you know why you're seeing me for marriage counseling? There's one fundamental problem."

When he said, "I know what the problem is," I said, "Yeah, you think it's sitting outside this office."

He agreed, "Well, yeah, if she'd just.... Just give me two or three things quick, Brother Schaap. I don't want to take up a bunch of your time."

I said, "We're not going to fix your marriage in two or three quick anything. You're too interested in arriving somewhere. You're going to miss the whole journey."

I am not trying to get Dr. Johnny Colsten anywhere.

How could I possibly know where he's supposed to wind up? He was leading before I was out of diapers. When the Colstens came to First Baptist Church to serve God under the leadership of Brother Hyles, I was four years old.

The day after I became pastor, Mrs. Plopper celebrated her fortieth anniversary of working on the First Baptist Church staff. That means that I was a three year old when she started working on our staff. I'm supposed to come on this staff and lead them? Yes, because I've been given *exousia* authority over Mrs. Plopper, and she graciously obeys my authority. Ten thousand times more than I'm happy that I have *exousia* authority over a woman who was working here when I was three, I am more interested in having the Spirit of God to help her to do the job she's been doing since before I was out of diapers. I want to help people.

I'm not some demagogue who says, "I know what's going on here. I'm going to tell you what to do." That's why the moment I became pastor of First Baptist Church, I wrote down several things I wanted to accomplish. The first item on that list was, "God, if I become the pastor, I want to do something nice for Brother and Mrs. Colsten because he has been a rock holding our church together during this time of grief." That's why the Colstens went to Hawaii. Is that their destination? What's God's will for Brother Colsten? I don't know. Just keep doing what he's doing, and don't stop.

I have great dreams and hopes for First Baptist Church, but no person coming in at 43 years of age with no pastoral experience is going to lead in the same way Brother Hyles did. He had a great feel for it, and I have tremendous confidence the future of this church is going to be nothing but great. I believe that as much as I know I'm saved. Recently, I told you the story about meeting with Brother Hyles and telling him the one reason I did not want to become the next pastor of First Baptist Church of Hammond. My reason was that of all the so-called great churches that had been taken over by the next man, none were doing very well. After some thought on the subject, he agreed with me.

When my wife and I got into the car to drive home after that service, I said, "I don't think I should have said that to the congregation."

She said, "You're right. You probably don't want to remind the people that what is happening here has never been done before, and it's probably not a real confidence builder to the people to think it's not going to continue to happen."

I said, "The truth of the matter is, it is happening." The mezzanine had to be opened for the Memorial Day weekend, and it's been open every Sunday since, and it never has before. We don't know where to put the college kids when they come; the college enrollment is up. The finances have been outstanding. We were 150% over our budget today. The church members have all stepped up the pace. Souls are being saved; baptisms are incredible. It's happening! Not because I hold *exousia* power, not because I'm the pastor, but because a whole lot of First Baptist Church members have realized it doesn't matter who holds the title. What matters is do we love those who walk through our doors.

It doesn't matter who holds the position. Are we growing because Mr. Cuozzo is the choir director? Are we growing because Dr. Colsten is the associate pastor? Are we growing because Dr. Sisson is the Hammond Baptist Grade School principal? Are we growing because Dr. Lapina is our youth director? Is this ministry growing because Bob Marshall joined the church staff? The truth of the matter is, churches don't grow because of *exousia* power; they grow because of *dunamis* power. First Baptist Church is not growing because I am the pastor. It is growing because the Spirit of the living God is exercising *dunamis* power to those who don't care about position, but are caring about those under the position.

Do you want a great family? Stop worrying about the title you hold and start earning the right to hold it. Want to have a great marriage? Stop worrying about, "Give me two or three quick things to fix my marriage."

We're on a journey together. That's all I did. I walked up alongside Brother Colsten and said, "You and I both know I've been given a different title here, but let's just put our shoulder to the burden, and let me help you carry the burden now."

I said to Ray Young, "Ray, we're both dying inside. I lost a father-in-law and boss, and you lost your buddy. You were close to Brother Hyles in a rare way, and I'm really sorry, but why don't we just pick up the burden together, and let's push it together?"

I said to Brother Eddie Lapina, "Brother Eddie, the church trusted you and made you business manager. Why don't you just stay there and help me? I don't know what I'm doing. Why don't you help me run the finances, and I'll serve you and you serve me."

I told somebody in his presence the other day, "Brother Eddie and I will never have a cross word. We do a lot of work together because of the financial load of the whole ministry. We spend a lot of time together and work, but I'll never have a cross word with him because I've agreed already I'm going to get along with him."

I want to get along with all of my staff. Why? I haven't earned the right to cross them. Maybe ten years from now I'll have earned that right. Even if I felt now that I had earned the right I wouldn't do it. Why? That's *exousia*; in fact, that's insecure *exousia*. It is *exousia* that is scared it might lose its *exousia*.

[196]

I wasn't looking for *exousia* when I was voted in as pastor of First Baptist Church of Hammond. I was at the college where Brother Hyles put me. When he asked me to be vice president, I said, "If you want me to, I will."

He said, "I want you to." That's why I ran away from the topic of pastoring every time he talked about it. Why? I wasn't candidating for it.

I wasn't looking for *exousia*, but I said, "God, I'm scared that vote's going to go the way I believe it's going to go; and if it happens, I don't want the position. I want to love those people like they have been cared for and loved for 41 years. That's what I want to give them. I want to give them my heart."

Mom and Dad, are you catching on? Would you go home and say, "What I want is for those who call me, 'Dad,' to know they've been loved by a man who loves them. What I want is a wife to feel loved by a man who loves her. I don't know where my marriage is going to wind up."

Mrs. Hyles felt much loved by her husband, and the grief she feels now is that that love, as strong as it was, has been removed from her presence. However impressed she had been with the fact that her husband held an *exousia* position, I promise you ten thousand times she was ten thousand times more impressed that he had *dunamis* love. The Spirit of God moved mightily in that man.

Brother Hyles' *dunamis* love is what drew people to him. People would come to First Baptist Church and say, "He doesn't look real impressive." Often in a sermon he would talk about, "I don't look like your idea of the pastor of the world's largest church." You might have been impressed with his position. Many of you shook and trembled in his presence because he was the pastor of the world's largest Sunday school, but what knocked your socks off was not his position, but his *dunamis* love.

[197]

Exousia may impress for a little bit. *Exousia* may bring admiration and honor. *Exousia* may have somebody get you to sign his Bible. *Exousia* may get attention the first week or two in the classroom. *Exousia* may get people to call you "Miss" or "Mr. So- and-So." *Exousia* may get you a title. *Exousia* might get you a business card. *Exousia* might get you letterhead with your name on it. *Exousia* might make you honored and respected in certain circles, but *exousia* won't put one soul in Heaven. *Exousia* won't build one bus route. *Exousia* won't fix one marriage. *Exousia* won't build one teenager's life. *Exousia* hasn't done one thing. *Exousia* is sought by a whole bunch of pompous, arrogant, cocky, proud people.

It's *dunamis* that changes a life! It's the power of God saying, "I love you, and I don't care about position." *Dunamis* says, "I just want you to know I love you." *"But ye shall receive power,"* is *dunamis*—if the Holy Ghost has come upon you.

Young preacher boys, stop worrying about where you'll preach, what pulpit you'll hold, what title you'll have. Make sure you've got the right Bible, and make sure you walk humbly with your God. Practice walking in and out of your auditorium. Practice sitting in your chair. I do both because Brother Hyles said he did. On Saturday night, get on your face behind your pulpit and pray something like this, "Oh God, tomorrow I preach here. Oh, my God, the man who stood here loved these people. My position does not impress them. God, help me to love these people. Love them through me."

Young preacher boy, it's not *exousia* you need; it's *dunamis* you need. It's not position you need; it's a mighty baptism of the Spirit of God. Bus captain, those bus kids don't need an *exousia* bus captain; they need a *dunamis* bus captain. They need someone to love them who's more concerned about loving and giving and caring.

Mom and Dad, if you'd be a *dunamis* parent instead of an *exousia* parent, it would revolutionize your home. My daughter is 20 years old, and I don't make her decisions for her. I make myself available for her. The time will come when I'll have to say good-bye to her. The time will come when I have to walk her down the aisle and give her away. I know that. She's not going to be impressed that I had *exousia* power. What will matter to my daughter when I give her away is, "Daddy, I felt your love. You were there for me. We had something special. We're buddies and pals. I trust you, Dad. I love you, Dad. I want to build a home just like you have, Dad."

My daughter told me several years ago, "Dad, my goal is to build a home just like you and mom have given Kenny and me." I cannot tell you how I cried. I said, "God, how does a man feel happier than I feel right now? What greater tribute could I have?"

Did she say, "I want to marry a man who has a position like you"? No, she said, "I want a home like you and mom gave me."

I've said to married couples with whom I counsel, "I know you have all the answers, and I know you come to me and say, 'Brother Schaap, that doesn't work. Give me two or three quick things.' All I could wish is that you'd have a marriage like I have. I wish you could have a marriage like I watched my in-laws have." They loved each other where *dunamis* power was much more prevalent than *exousia* power. Bus captain, Sunday school teacher, husband, wife, mother, father, schoolteacher, staff member—whatever *exousia* position you have is quite meaningless unless you have *dunamis* power—the power to influence, the power to love—the power that causes people to say, "That person made all the difference in the world."

That's why Pam Hibbard, whose position is teacher at City Baptist High School, probably has more people she's influenced because she learned a long time ago it's *dunamis* that makes the difference. That's why some who do not have high positions have literally changed hundreds and hundreds of peoples' lives. A long time ago they realized they wanted the mighty power of God, and that is to influence lives within the position they have been given. To the person who gives all the *dunamis* he can at the level where he is, God just might give him more *exousia* to pave the way for him to give more *dunamis* at a higher level.

I never dreamed I would be voted in as the pastor of First Baptist Church of Hammond, Indiana; but when I preached at the rest home or jail, I gave it all I had. The first time I preached I was 17 years old. I preached to my home church youth group at Rose Park Baptist Church in Holland, Michigan. I preached to a dozen or so of my peers. When I finished, my pastor said, "Wow, you really meant business, didn't you?"

I said, "Well, I had a lot on my heart. I prayed and studied a long time. I love those kids."

Brother Hyles said it many times, and I agree with him, "I do not have to offer what somebody else may have to offer, but I can give all that I do have, and so can you." Stop worrying about the position you have, and give all the *dunamis* you can within the realm of *exousia* that God has given you. That's what I truly want from the Holy Spirit.

CHAPTER ELEVEN

"Thou Hast Asked a Hard Thing: Nevertheless"

■   ■   ■

II Kings 2:8-14 says, *"And Elijah took his mantle, and wrapped it together, and smote the waters, and they were divided hither and thither, so that they two went over on dry ground. And it came to pass, when they were gone over, that Elijah said unto Elisha, Ask what I shall do for thee, before I be taken away from thee. And Elisha said, I pray thee, let a double portion of thy spirit be upon me. And he said, Thou hast asked a hard thing: nevertheless, if thou see me when I am taken from thee, it shall be so unto thee; but if not, it shall not be so. And it came to pass as they still went on, and talked, that, behold, there appeared a chariot of fire, and horses of fire, and parted them both-er asunder; and Elijah went up by a whirlwind into heaven. And Elisha saw it, and he cried, My father, my father, the chariot of Israel, and the horsemen thereof. And he saw him no more: and he took hold of his own clothes, and rent them in two pieces. He took up also the mantle of Elijah that fell from him, and went back, and stood by the bank of Jordan; And he took the mantle of Elijah that fell from him, and smote the waters, and said, Where is the LORD God of Elijah? and when he also had smitten the waters, they parted hither and thither: and Elisha went over."*

I want to use the story of Elijah and Elisha to remind us just a little bit about what our purpose here at First Baptist Church is on the near-anniversary of Brother Hyles' leaving us to go to Heaven.

I'm sure there were at least two hundred letters I got shortly after I became pastor and throughout the first year, where people reminded me of the great stories of the Bible where people like Elijah would go to Heaven, and a ministry continued and flourished to even greater heights, as it did under Elisha. People would say, "Remember Moses and Joshua." Moses did incredible one-of-a-kind works that nobody could ever duplicate. Yet, Joshua was privileged to do some things that even Moses was not allowed to do.

They reminded me of the stories of David and Solomon. David, the great warrior king who fought the great battles, and destroyed the Philistines was attacked again and again with much false criticism against him; yet, a marvelous, marvelous Christian. Yet, he was succeeded by a man who built great works, and took the kingdom of David to heights that had never before been dreamed of, almost dizzying heights.

Each of these situations—Elijah with Elisha, Moses and Joshua, David and Solomon, and others you can think of in the Bible—each are wonderful testimonies that God often and regularly and frequently is reminding us that a ministry never has to end because the one-of-a-kind, singular, unique man passes off the scene. That's very important for us to know, and I remind you of that often. That is the theme here, because it's important that we don't become infected with the disease that infected so many other big ministries—these mega ministries that were pastored by men of charisma and charm. Nobody had Brother Hyles' wit. Nobody had his quick mind. Nobody had his charm and his poise. Nobody had his preaching ability. Nobody had his leadership skills. Nobody had his administrative skills, and yet, we can't sit there in a corner, and suck our thumb, and say, "I guess we can't go on."

The truth of the matter is, to the chagrin of many of our friends and even some of our enemies out here, they have been a bit astonished at how you have risen as a mighty army, and have done great works.

I said when I became pastor that no man could fill Brother Hyles' shoes, but all of us stepping in those shoes together could fill them, and you have done that nobly.

The ministry of Elijah and Elisha is really interesting. Elijah performed six miracles. He took a barrel of meal and a cruse of oil, barely enough for one meal for a widow and her son, and for many, many weeks and months it never ran empty. She would look inside the barrel, and the meal would be just a handful, and the cruse of oil would have just a half cup full, but she'd pour it out, and back inside would be a little bit of meal and a little bit of oil. It never exhausted itself.

Then, he healed that widow's son. I can't be certain that he died, but he came pretty close to it. He was near death, and Elijah raised him up to life. Then, he built the altar on Mount Carmel. He challenged the 400 prophets of Baal and the 450 associate prophets of Baal. He called down the fire of God in a 63 word prayer, and brought great deliverance to the nation of Israel in a contest against Ahab's false prophets.

Then, he prayed, and it did not rain. He prayed again, and it rained. There was a three-year interlude. He prayed for a drought, and it didn't rain for three and a half years. He prayed that it would rain, and the rains came in a huge deluge.

He prophesied against Ahab and Jezebel and told specifically how they would die, and how the dogs would lick the blood of Ahab when he died in a chariot, and how the dogs would literally eat the body of Jezebel, and both of those prophesies came true a short time after.

He was on a mountain when two captains plus their fifty men came to snatch him, and seize him, and he said, *"If I be a man of God, then let fire come down from heaven, and consume thee and thy fifty."* (II Kings 1:10b) One hundred and two men died in answer to the word of Elijah.

He prophesied that a double portion of his ministry could rest upon his successor, Elisha, and that's exactly what happened. The last act he committed was to part the Jordan River, and then go into Heaven.

Six miracles and two prophesies! Elisha was with Elijah right at the time of that last big event of the parting of the Jordan River. Elijah says, "You know I have to leave you soon."

He said, "I know that."

Elijah said, "We may not have a chance to talk again. Is there anything you would want me to do for you?"

He said, "Yes, there is."

Elijah said, "What would you like me to do for you?"

He said, "I'd like a double portion of what you have."

I love the next line, *"Thou hast asked a hard thing: nevertheless."* Elisha's ministry consists of twelve miracles and four prophesies, exactly double of what Elijah had done.

The first thing he did is he copied the last thing his predecessor did: he parted the Jordan River. Next, he healed some poisonous water that was killing some people. Next, he prophesied in the middle of a drought that there would be water that would fill all the ditches the people could dig. He told them, "You dig all the ditches, and every ditch you dig will be filled with water," and it happened as he prophesied.

He told the widow lady, who was bankrupt and whose husband had died and had left her with no insurance and no money, "Get all the vessels you can. Borrow not a few, and just get them here." They were miraculously filled with oil, and she took and sold the oil, and paid off all her debts, and was pretty well-to-do.

He healed a Shunammite's son, a boy who had died in his mother's arms, and he raised him back to life. This was a boy that had been given in answer to the prayer and prophesy of Elisha.

He healed the poisonous pottage. Brother Hyles preached a sermon called, "There's Poison in the Pot," and Elisha healed the poison that was in the pot.

He miraculously fed 100 men. It was very similar to how Jesus fed the 5,000. He took 20 loaves of bread, and fed 100 men in a miraculous feeding. He healed Naaman the leper, who was the great, famous general of the army of Syria. He healed that man so his skin was like that of a new-born baby.

He recovered the lost axe head for a preacher boy, who had borrowed an axe to build a college dormitory and was afraid he couldn't keep his school bill paid if he didn't get that axe head. Elisha put a stick in the water. The Bible says the iron swam right to the surface, and he grabbed it. It's an amazing little story.

He revealed the secret military plans of the Syrian general. He was getting old and couldn't see very well, but he called the Israeli army general. He said, "Syria's going to come this way, and they're going to have these battle plans."

"How do you know that?"

"Trust me." The Israeli general trusted and was waiting in ambush.

The Syrian general said to his men, "Which one of you is a traitor?"

"Nobody," they responded.

"Well, how is this happening?"

"They've got a man of God in that city. His name is Elisha, and God's reading your plans and telling an angel; and the angel is telling that prophet, and he's telling the general." They ended the war because of that.

He opened the eyes of his servant to see the armies of God in the Heavens. His servant, Gahazi, was nervous about the coming Syrian war, and Elisha said, "What are you worried about?"

He said, "Well, there's more soldiers out there than we have," and Elisha said, "No! There are more on our side than are against us!"

"What do you mean?"

Elisha said, "Go outside, look up to the heavens, and I'll show you what I'm talking about." He looked up and saw the chariots of God, and the horsemen; twenty thousand chariots of fire waiting to come down."

He walked back inside, and said, "How'd you know that?"

Elisha said, "I walk by faith, not like you do. I know these things."

Elisha smote the Syrians with blindness. There was a whole army of Syrians, and Elisha walked out and said, "God, give them blindness." He then said, "Follow me, fellows, and I'll take you to safety," and he marched them right into the POW camp.

The Israeli president said, "Should I kill them?"

Elisha said, "Kill them? Give them a good meal, and send them home," and that ended another war with Syria.

He prophesied the arrival of food during the Syrian siege. They had been in such a great famine, and the Syrians were compassed about, and people were selling the dung of birds. People would buy it because they were so hungry, and

Elisha said, "Tomorrow you're going to be eating bread and eating good food." They laughed at him, and he said, "It will happen," and it did.

Then he prophesied the seven-year famine, and he prophesied Hazael's reign of Syria. Hazael was a servant to king Ben-hadad. He told Hazael, "You're a wicked man, and you're going to kill your leader and become the king of Syria," which he did.

Then, after Elisha was dead, there was a band of Moabites running through the land. They were being chased by the policemen. They took a body of a man they had killed, and they said, "Hey, there's an empty tomb over there. Just throw this guy's body in there, and let's get out of here before the police catch us." They threw the man in there, and his body hit the decaying bones of Elisha, and the victim resurrected from the dead. The police did not catch them, I guarantee you that! They made tracks! Elisha performed 11 miracles in his lifetime, and God allowed an extra one after his death.

Exactly double. Elijah—six miracles and two prophesies; Elisha—twelve miracles and four prophesies, a double portion.

I have been consumed of where I believe this church could be. I've been consumed literally from the time I became pastor. I've been consumed with what I know we're capable of doing, and what I believe we should do. I'm consumed with the fact that it would be the mistake of a century, perhaps the greatest mistake in the history of Christendom, if this church were to falter and fail, and to stagnate and maintain.

This church is sitting on a precipice from which we can leap and become like so many other churches who failed to seize their opportunity or we can go to new heights, and show the whole nation that we have caught what Brother

Hyles taught and what our Saviour commanded.

I get consumed when I realize what you're capable of doing. I've never wanted anything more in my life than to take the ministry Brother Hyles left behind and meet him someday and have us all greet him and have him say, "You did it! You did what I taught."

I want to talk to you about this business of a double portion. I'm going to talk straight from the heart.

First of all, I believe we ought to ask God for something hard. I think we ought to ask God to do something hard for us. *"Thou hast asked a hard thing."* I like that. I personally believe that not too many people make God sweat too hard. I don't think God has to roll up His sleeves and work very hard for very many Christians. There are very few people who ask God to do very much of anything.

You college students think you're taxing God's ability because you need $100 on your school bill, or you need a job, or you need the grace of God to stay at Americall, or because you have a hard time driving to Overnight Express, or because you have a cussing boss who uses vulgar language when he describes your work ethic, or lack thereof.

God must sit up in Heaven almost drawing unemployment because Christians refuse to make Him do anything hard. I'm talking about the God who parted the Red Sea. Folks, how many times have you seen Lake Michigan parted? I've walked on it, but I've never parted it.

This is the God we're dealing with—the God Who built this church. We sometimes wonder if God can see us through a tough time. We pray as we should, and we agonize as we probably should about medical tests. We wonder if God can see us through the loss of a loved one. We agonize whether God can help us with a house payment or a car payment. We wonder if God is big enough to help us find a nice house for our family. We agonize whether we can make it through final exams. We breathe a sigh of relief and say, "There must be a God in Heaven, I got a "C" on an English test," and God must say, "What? That was hard?"

God must be waiting for somebody somewhere sometime in His lifetime where He says, "Now, that's a hard one. That's a tough one." I want to be the one who makes God say that. I want to be one human being, that in God's lifetime, He looks at me when I meet him, and will say, "You rascal, you put Me to the test." I want Him to say, "Cottonpick, Jack, you made Me roll up my sleeves, and I even broke a sweat coming through for you."

The only time you find God resting is after He worked, and that is in Genesis chapters one and two. God never again had to take a rest over anything anybody asked Him to do. Do you think after He got those people across the Red Sea that He was sweating and saying, "I've got to rest"? There's not one mention of God resting after He parted the Red Sea. There's not one mention of God resting after He parted the Jordan River. There's not one mention of His resting after He helped feed the five thousand. There's not one mention of His resting when He gave water from a flint rock. If it came from limestone, it would have been natural and easy, but it came from a flint rock. Sparks were flying from the top while water was flowing from the side. God was saying, "I just thought I'd show you I can do it even if it seems unnatural and impossible."

God is so eager to show how strong He is. The bottom line is, I don't think anybody's ever put Him to the test. After He's finished all of the Old Testament, God says, "Here's what I did. Elijah called down fire from Heaven, and I spit fire out, but I didn't rest after Elijah called fire down from Heaven." Elijah rested, but God didn't rest. He says, "After I fed the children of Israel manna for 40 years, when I had to rain it down from Heaven and put it on the frost; after I gave the quail, that did not exist in the desert—and I brought in billions. I don't care if scientists say you can't do it—I did it." He says, "Name Me one thing in the Bible that I couldn't come through and do. Every time My people's backs were up against the wall, didn't I come through? Name Me one time in the Word of God where I ever sat down after somebody asked Me to do something, and I said, 'That sure was hard.'"

He said, "The only time it was hard was when I took nothing, and I made the heavens. I put every planet from Pluto to Mars out there. I created Earth. I put the waters and the dinosaurs in their places. I placed the heavens. I flung the stars into space. Your man might put a shuttle of astronauts into space orbit, but the furthest you've gone is the moon, and the furthest you've put a piece of machinery is just past one tiny planet named Pluto. I've got billions of universes out there, and the only time I got a little tired is after I created all of it in six days. I sat back and said, 'That was hard.'"

I want to be the church, and I want to be the pastor, and I want to be the people that God says, "You want what?"

Like the story of a man walking along a beach, and he finds an Aladdin's lamp, and he picks up the lamp, and rubs it. The genie comes out, and the genie says, "You get one wish."

He said, "Well, what about my three wishes. I thought I would get three?"

The genie said, "You get one."

He said, "I want three."

The genie said, "Shut up. I'll give you one or you won't get any."

He said, "Okay, my wife and I want to go to Hawaii on a honeymoon, but I get seasick. I want you to build me a highway from California to Hawaii."

[210]

The genie said, "That's a stupid wish. I can't do it. Name me another one."

He said, "Look, you're a genie. You can do anything. I want you to build me a highway from California to Hawaii."

The genie said, "I can't do that. It's impossible. Give me something else."

He said, "Good night, you're a genie. I found you, I rubbed the lamp, you came out, and I get a wish. It's bad enough I don't get two more. I get one stupid wish, and I want a highway from here to Hawaii."

The genie said, "I told you I can't do that. Now give me something else; otherwise, I'm leaving you here without granting you any wishes."

He said, "Okay, okay." Thoughtfully the man pondered his one wish, and then looked at the genie and stated, "I want you to help me understand women."

The genie thought and thought for a while and then answered, "Was that a two-lane or a four-lane highway you wanted?"

I want to go to God, and for God to say, "It's too hard. Ask for something else!" I want to nag Him, and nag Him, and finally get Him to say, "Okay, you can have what you want, but I'll have to work at that."

I want God to roll up His sleeves for some church and say, "Wow! You have asked a hard thing. This will take all I've got. This will take My omnipotence; but, I'll do it for you." I want something difficult. I want something real. I want something genuine. I want something where God steps back and says, "Let Me rest a minute. That was a hard request. *Thou hast asked a hard thing.*'"

Hard thing? Double what you've done? Elijah says, "Do you know what I've done? I've done six miracles that have never been done before. I've had two prophesies come true. Nobody has ever done that. I've called fire down out of heaven in a 63-word prayer. I took 850 prophets of Baal, and I killed those rascals. I stamped out Baalism. I put Ahab on the run. God has used me!"

Elisha said, "Okay, I want twice as much."

"Twice as much?"

"Yes, if your God's big enough to do six miracles for you, and answer two prophesies that you've uttered out of your mouth, then I want twelve miracles and four prophesies, and I want everything you had and twice as much."

God must have been standing up in Heaven saying, "Shut up a minute. I've got a guy down there who wants Me. I've got somebody down there that needs Me. I've got somebody down there who believes I can do twice as much as I've ever done for anybody in the whole Bible."

That's how Joshua felt when he said, "I'm succeeding Moses? He parted the Red Sea. What can I do?" God says, "Let's tear down the walls of Jericho. Let's part the Jordan River when it's swelling over. Let's go in that land right there, and you won't ever have to shoot an arrow out of the bow. All you've got to do is walk around the city six times, and then seven times on the seventh day, and all you've got to do is shout and say, 'Glory to God,' and the walls will come tumbling down." Joshua said, "That'll work."

God is looking for somebody who will make Him break out in a sweat. God's looking for somebody to ask, "Would anybody like a double portion? Anybody want to see twice as much as you've seen before? Anybody want to see it where everybody steps back and says, 'We ain't ever seen it like that before.'"

We find at the end of the Old Testament, as God has said, "I parted the Red Sea. I created the heavens and the earth. I brought manna to My people. I've fed them water out of a flint rock. I've brought billions of quail to feed the millions of people. For 40 years I moved that rock, and it followed them through the sand; that Rock was Christ. I protected them with a pillar of cloud by day, and a pillar of fire by night. I was a wall of fire unto them. I've performed miracle after miracle after miracle."

Malachi 3:10 says, *"...prove me now herewith..."* He said, "I've looked for thirty-nine books for somebody to tell Me that I'm needed to do twice as much as anybody's ever done, but I haven't found anybody. Would somebody please rise up and say, 'I dare you, God, to come through. I dare you, God, to step in. I dare you, God, to do twice as much. I dare you for a double portion. I dare you to double my bus route. I dare you to double the size of this congregation. I dare you to double my Sunday school class. I dare you to double my soul winning for this next year.'"

I wonder if God's ever said to anybody, "Wow, that's a hard one. I don't know if I can do that. You're asking Me something that's going to take a mighty big God to do that." That will take the God who only one time in His entire recorded book said, "I had to rest after I did that."

Do you think a God who insists you work hard is afraid of hard work? Do you think God is a lazy God? God's a hard-working God, and God said, "I believe nobody's ever asked Me to do anything too hard for Me. In fact, I wrote in Genesis 18:14, "Is any thing too hard for the Lord?"

I wish one of you fellows, who are about to graduate, would say to God, "Yes, God, I want You to help me start a church in a tough area. I want to go someplace where it's never been done before, and I want to build a church for the glory of God." But I'm afraid I hear God saying, "You can't even pass your English test. You can't even make your bed. You can't even get along with your girlfriend."

I wish somebody would be like Daniel, Shadrach, or Meschach who were ten times better than the next best. I wish somebody would be like Elisha, and say, "I want a double portion of your spirit." I wish every Sunday school teacher would say, "I want to double my Sunday school class this year." I wish every Sunday school superintendent would say, "I'm going to double the size of my department this next year."

I wish some bus captain would get excited, and say, "I'm going to double the size of my bus route this year." I wish some Bible Club leader would get excited and say, "By the grace of God, I'm going to double the size of my Bible Club this year."

I wish every soul-winning club in this church would double its attendance, and double the number of converts they get saved this year. I wish every soul winner would say, "I want to double the number of converts I win to Christ, and I want to double the baptisms I see in the baptistery."

I wish our homeless ministry would say, "I want to double the number of the homeless we bring to church on Sunday morning." I wish our Gospel League Home workers would say, "I want to double the number of ladies and children who come from the Gospel League Home in Chicago."

I wish our nursing home ministry would say, "Instead of averaging 125 this year, we want to average 250." I wish our Spanish Department running 300-500 more each week than they did last year would say, "That's nothing. That's too easy for God. We want to make it hard for you, God. Let's double the size of our Spanish Department."

I wish our Deaf Department wouldn't say, "Boy, wasn't our fortieth anniversary wonderful? We had over 400 on a big day." Why don't you go for 500 or 600 or 700?

Why don't you pull out all the stops and say, "God, we're going to ask a very hard thing. We want to do something that's never been done like it before."

I wish our Rescue Mission would double in size. I wish our Blind Department would hunt down every person who is hard of seeing or blind and needs help, and beg and plead, and double the size of that department. I wish our Pathfinder Department would double its size so they overflow that beautiful new building they've been given. I wish our Sunbeam Department would likewise have to ask for more space because there's so many handicapped children that more room is needed.

I wish the Truck Stop Ministry would double in size until we have a whole section filled with truck drivers. I wish our Sailor Ministry would double its size. You're doing a great job, and I know your difficulties, but let's believe God for great growth.

Is there anything too hard for God? Where is the God of Elijah? Where is the God of Moses? Where is the God of Joshua? Where is the God of Christ Almighty? Where is the God, Who says, "Hey, why don't you ask Me something hard to do?"

I wish every adult Sunday school teacher would say, "I'm tired of running 50, 60, 70, 80, or 100, 150, or 200. I want it jam-packed. I want to go to Brother Schaap, and nag him like an unhappy woman for more space. I want to stretch it out and build bigger and nag him until we get a bigger room." Why? "Because we're doubling the size of our class this year."

I wish Teenage Soul Winning would double the number of teenagers and the number of converts. I wish Hammond Baptist Schools would get excited and double the number of school students. I want those schools bulging at the sides. I want to have to go to the deacons and say, "I don't know where to put all the kids. We've got to build bigger gymnasiums and more classrooms, and hire more teachers. We just don't know where to put them." Bless God, let's train a generation to rise up in righteousness for God.

I wish Hyles-Anderson College was running 5,000 students. I want to tell you why. Two years ago last month Brother Mike Fish was cutting Brother Hyles' hair in his office. He was his barber, and he was cutting Brother Hyles' hair just a few days before Brother Hyles was stricken and had to go to the hospital. Brother Hyles said, "Brother Mike, how's your work doing?" Brother Mike is in charge of student recruitment at our college. Brother Mike was asking some questions, and Brother Hyles said, "You know, Brother Mike, there's no reason our college shouldn't be running 5,000 kids."

Brother Mike Fish said, "Brother Hyles, that's an amazing thing. How would you do that?"

Brother Hyles said, "Let me think that over. That's a very good question. I'll get back to you next time we meet." They never met again. Brother Mike Fish told me that story just a few weeks ago in my office. He was cutting my hair. When you left my office, Brother Mike, my heart beat inside my breast, and I said, "To the glory of God, and for the memory of Brother Hyles, why is our college not running that many? Hundreds of our graduates are out there, and tens of thousands of potential students are out there. They're going to all of the state universities, and becoming everything but a preacher boy." Bless God, let's rally the cry of our graduates. Let's get these young people trained. We'll send them back to you as assistant pastors and soul-winning laymen. Let's train a generation to rise up, so God says, "Wow! Even I never thought I could do that."

I want God to one day say in Heaven, "You know what? There was a generation one time on the earth, and they put Me to the test. I didn't know I could do what I did, but I did it! I sweated, and I rolled up my sleeves, and said, 'Look what We did together.'"

I want God to see how big He is. I want God to know how strong He is. The Bible says in II Chronicles 16:9, *"For the eyes of the LORD run to and fro throughout the whole earth, to shew himself strong...."* God says, "I'm not sure I know how strong I am because I've never met anybody who's willing to test My strength."

"How big a barbell can You pick up, God?"

God says, "Every one I've tried, I've picked up. How big of a one have you got?"

"God, how fast can You throw that football?"

God says, "Every football I've picked up, I've passed it. Which one do you want Me to pass?"

"God, how wide a river have You ever parted?"

He said, "The biggest is the Jordan. It was swollen over."

"What's the biggest body of water?"

"The Red Sea."

"How big a body of water could You part?"

"I don't know. Those are the only two anybody's ever needed Me or asked Me to part."

"How big of a church can You build, God?"

"Well, the biggest I've ever built is in Hammond. You're sitting in it."

"How big a church could you build?"

"I don't know. That's the only one anybody's asked Me to build."

"How big a Sunday school could You build?"

"I don't know. Nobody's asked Me much to help them build their Sunday school. They want Me to bless them, but they don't know what that means. They don't want a double portion. They just want to keep it maintained."

I don't want to maintain anything. I don't want status quo. I don't want things as they are. I want to sweat and I want God to sweat. "God, I want You to roll up Your sleeves. God, I want You to work so hard You've got to say, 'Time out. I need a break. I've got to sit down and rest a little while. Time out. I need to bring you up in the Rapture. I'm getting too old for this.' "

Anybody think like I do? Anybody wonder how big a class you could build? How big a bus route? How big a Bible club you could build? How big this church could grow? Anybody wonder how much we could pack in that new auditorium? I wish we could get in that new auditorium, and the first Sunday say, "Oops, too small!"

One Monday and Tuesday I flew out of town with Brother Hyles. We flew out of O'Hare and came back and rushed to the college. He preached, then he drove me back to the church because my car was here. As we left the college, we were driving together, and he said to me, "You know, if I wasn't 63 years of age, I'd build me a 7,500-seat auditorium, and fill it."

I said, "Why don't you?"

He looked at me, and he patted my leg, and he said, "Because the next fool who has to take over this ministry will have to pay the bills and fill it."

I said, "Why are you looking at me that way?"

He said, "Just in case you know any fool who's going to do it."

I said, "I don't know what you're talking about."

He said, "You mark my words, boy, I'd do it. I'd build me a 7,500-seat auditorium, and I'd fill it. What do you think you could do?"

I said, "I could be a real good teacher at Hyles-Anderson College."

We're building that auditorium over there because that's what he'd said he'd do, and I'm not going to go to Heaven some day, and wonder if I could have or should have or would have. I'm going to do it."

Let's keep singing the song, "Our Best." Do you know what? I hate that song. I hate "best." I like doing it. Best is a cop-out for people who are too lazy to say, "I don't know what my best is." You have never known what your best is. There's not one person who knows what his best is.

I think often of the story from World War II. It was Omaha Beach, the thick of the fighting, the first twenty-four hours our G.I.'s were crawling on that beach and trying to make it to a hole to keep from getting killed. Those first few hours they weren't thinking about fighting Nazi Germany all the way to Berlin; they were trying their best to keep from being pushed back in the sea, and dying, and losing tens of thousands of men. Five thousand men died on that beach within twenty-four hours. It was the first few minutes; the Germans had murderous firepower. They had lined up their mortars, and zeroed in their guns for a withering cross fire. Hundreds of men were falling. Big, huge bunkers of solid concrete reinforced with steel had to be knocked out.

One of the leaders, a lieutenant or captain, called one of the engineers over and said, "Do you know how to blow up that thing?"

He said, "Yes, I do."

The leader said, "Go blow it up."

"I'll do my best, sir."

"That a boy!" The engineer got shot and killed. The leader said, "Give me another engineer." Another engineer came over, and the leader said, "Son, do you know how to blow up that bunker?"

He said, "Yes, I do."

The leader said, "Go blow it up."

"Yes sir, I'll do my best."

"That a boy!" That engineer got shot and killed. The leader said, "Give me another engineer." A third man came over, and the same story repeated. The leader said, "Son, I want you to go and blow up that bunker right there."

He said, "Yes sir, I'll give it my best."

"That a boy!" That engineer got shot and killed. The leader said, "Give me another engineer," and a fourth man came over, and he asked him, "Do you know how to blow that thing up?"

He said, "I think so."

The leader said, "Can you do it?"

He said, "Yes, sir. I'll do my best."

The leader said, "No, you're not going to do your best. There are three dead men that gave their best. I want you to blow up that stupid thing right now before any more men die giving it their best. I don't care about your best. Blow it up!" That engineer also died, but he died blowing a massive hole in that concrete bunker and succeeded as commanded.

Every time I read that story I say, "God, I don't ever want to do my best. I want to do it." I don't know what my best is, but I guarantee you, a hundred times you've done what you've thought was your best, and God's said, "You haven't even broken stride. You haven't even broken a sweat." Your best is often far down from what God expects.

I'm afraid to go to Heaven and have God say, "Yeah, I saw your best." I want to go to Heaven, and say, "God, I don't know if it was my best or not, but we did it."

I'm not going to give it my best shot to build that auditorium. We're going to build it. I'm not going to try my hardest to fill it. We're going to fill it. I'm not going to be a bus captain that says, "I'm giving my best to this bus route." No, God, I'm going to take that bus and that money that's being spent, and I'm going to fill that bus, and put boys and girls on that bus.

I don't care what my best is or my worst is. You deserve my best. You deserve the job to get done.

God didn't say, "I'm going to give it my best try and create the heavens and the earth. Let's see how I can do." No, He did it.

Sometimes you don't know what your best is. I think it's a great song. Keep on singing it. Every time I sing it, I'm so convicted because I'm so afraid my best is really much further than what I think my best is.

I want a generation here to look at Brother Hyles someday when you see him in Heaven, and say, "Brother Hyles, not only did I catch what you taught, but I did it."

I want to ask God to do something that's very hard. I want our inner-city chapels to double. I want our mission board to double the number of missionaries we're sending out. I want our City Baptist Schools to double their size. I want our college to double its size. I want this ministry to grow and flex, and grow and flex, and grow and flex, where everybody is out working and sweating, and God is up in Heaven huffing and puffing, and saying, "Folks, would you please slow it down a notch? My angels are over-worked. I'm being charged double time and a half. I'm going broke up here in Heaven. I've exhausted every resource I've got. I don't have any more miracles to give you. I don't have any greater imagination. I've given you more souls than anybody has asked for. You folks, please knock it down a notch. We're flat out in Heaven. We're tired!" That's what I want!

I want to get God so frustrated He's forced to bring the Rapture. Then we can sit down and rest a little while.

How do you do that? How do you have a double portion?

1. **Get a double portion of the right spirit.** He didn't ask for twice as many miracles. He said, "I want a double portion of your spirit." He didn't say, "the Holy Spirit." He said, "your spirit."

God uses you to the degree you've got the right kind of spirit, the right attitude, and the right thinking.

Those of you who sat under Brother Hyles' ministry, I'd suggest you start acting like Brother Hyles. Those of you who say you're a dear, wonderful, godly friend of Brother Hyles, know his books, and love him, I suggest you start practicing Brother Hyles' ethics and Brother Hyles' justice and Brother Hyles' love for his enemies and Brother Hyles' standing for every preacher whether you agree with him or not. I'm suggesting you follow Brother Hyles' belief in not criticizing anybody. I suggest you understand, those who are good, godly people who all think you knew Brother Hyles well, it's time you understand this Book was Brother Hyles' favorite Book. The God he talked to was his favorite prayer partner. The work he did was his favorite work. It's time you entered into the spirit of the man you loved, the man you lived under, and the man you worshiped under. That man's spirit ought to permeate your home and your marriage. You ought to treat your wife like he treated his wife. You ought to treat your children like he treated his daughter. It's time you treat your people like he treated his people. It's time we catch the spirit of Brother Hyles.

All of the bickering, fussing, and feuding at home, and then saying, "God, bless my bus route," and God says, "Why should I? Your spirit stinks."

God's not going to double the size of Hammond Baptist Schools until every teacher captures the heart of the man who hired you. City Baptist Schools are not going to grow because we find you more money. It's going to grow because you find the right kind of spirit—the spirit of love, godliness, hard work, sweat, and sacrifice. That's what it is.

That building that's going to go up is going to be nothing more than a white elephant if it's not filled and run by people who caught the right spirit of Brother Hyles. It's not filled just because you knock on doors. It's filled by a God who blesses obedient people.

Brother Bob Marshall told me the other day, "Brother Schaap, I knocked on so many doors for my new Sunday school class, and had six couples committed to coming. Six, and only one couple came, but God gave me eight brand new couples I didn't even invite." Why? Because God does-n't build on your soul winning; God builds by blessing obedient people. When you go soul winning, God says, "I will build because you are obedient, but I'll do it My way to show you that I'm the One Who builds it."

Get out there and knock on doors. If you never get one person saved, be obedient. It's time you catch the fervent soul-winning spirit of Brother Hyles.

It's time you catch the passion for holiness that Brother Hyles had. It's time you get the passion, and do right. It's time God's people realize we've been given a golden opportunity, and that is to build a ministry the likes of which has never been seen in Christendom, but is built because we catch a double portion of the spirit of the man God used to build this church.

Yes, God used Brother Hyles to build this church. How did he do it? Because Brother Hyles opened wide his spirit and said, "God, they can criticize me. They can attack me, but I'm going to keep on working for You. Though they slay me, and though You slay me, yet will I trust in you."

Go ahead and write your dirty papers. Go ahead and blaspheme the man of God. Go ahead and criticize the work of God. I'm too busy winning souls, knocking on doors, helping the fallen, running the buses, raising the money, building the school, teaching boys how to preach, and too busy serving God to come down. Like Nehemiah said, "I'm doing a great work. I cannot come down." That's the spirit of Brother Hyles.

God knows we need a double portion of his spirit. It's time we understand that what we have available is not just a golden opportunity, but an opportunity that has never existed in Christian history. Not since Jesus said, "I will build my church," has there been anything like the First Baptist Church of Hammond, Indiana. Do you know what you're sitting in? History!

Brother Hyles used to say that when I was sitting on the platform, and I'd say, "God, I do know that. I do see that." For nearly 24 months, I have said, "God, I will never, never forget what I've been given."

Do you know what you've been given, folks? An opportunity, not just to coast along, and say, "Isn't it nice? We're not going downhill. Brother Schaap hasn't faltered too badly yet. God bless the poor sap. He's the young fool Brother Hyles was talking about."

No, folks, you're sitting as the teacher of a class that ought to double this year. You're driving a bus that ought to double this year.

I don't want to sit back and say, "Well, we grew five percent." I want to double! I want to say to Brother Hyles, "You taught us how to do it. Guess what we did?" He'll say, "I know what you've been doing, because I've been busting myself up here in Heaven. God's making me work overtime to help you down there." I want Brother Hyles to look over and say, "Wowie, Zowie! Look at those folks sweating away. God, look at that," and for God to say, "Shut up! I'm too busy helping them."

The book of Acts says over and over, "They were of one accord." They were all in one place. They were all together—the unity, the camaraderie, the togetherness, the teamwork. The spirit of the great prophet Elijah was in the spirit of Elisha—the spirit of teamwork, the spirit of cooperation, the spirit of sacrifice.

Don't you dare, for one minute, look at this church as an opportunity to say, "Boy, how much money could I make doing something in that new auditorium?" Get you a volunteer spirit.

2. Let's get a double portion of the works. When Elijah said, "What would you like?" Elisha said, "I'd like a double portion of your spirit." Elijah took his mantle off, and smote the waters. The first thing Elisha did afterwards was the same thing. He did the same work.

Jesus said in John 14:12, "*...the works that I do shall he do also; and greater works than these shall he do....*" Not greater in quality, but greater in quantity.

You can't do better works than getting a soul saved, and that's what Jesus was talking about, but instead of getting one saved, He wants you to get two saved. Instead of getting 20 saved, he wants you to get 40 saved.

"I've built my Sunday school class to 15," then let's go for 30. "I've got a bus route running 40," then let's go for 80.

Twelve years ago I became a bus captain of a little route in East Chicago, Indiana. I said to the bus driver, Don Mills, "Brother Mills, how long have you been driving this route?"

He said, "Well, I've been driving since the days of Wally Beebe, since about 1971 or 1972."

"What's the most people you've had on this route?"

"Well, I've probably had a dozen different bus captains. The biggest numbers we've had was 85 people."

This was February, and I said, "We'll break that in the Spring Program."

He said, "I don't think so."

I said, "Yes, we will." Two and a half months later, we had 87, then 114, then 117, then 230, and then 340. You see, I'm not content to say, "I'm going to break it a little bit. I don't want to just get by with what somebody else did."

I want God to look at this church and say, "You know what? I'm shocked. I knew I could do it, but I can't believe I did." I want God to look at you and say, "You know what? I thought you were a pretty decent Christian, but look at what you're doing." I want God to grab the angels and say, "Get over here. Look at what those people down in Hammond are doing. I've never seen it. I didn't dream it. I could not have conceived it. I never knew anybody would make Me work this hard."

I want God to say, *"Thou hast asked a hard thing: nevertheless."* Nevertheless what? You've got to catch the right spirit. Nevertheless what? You've got to keep doing the same works.

Ephesians 2:10 says, *"For we are his workmanship, created in Christ Jesus unto good works,"* Unto what? Good works. Not good feeling; good WORKS! This is not a charismatic church where we say, "I've got the feeling." Let's get out and work. I don't mind you praising God, but the way I praise God is to get out and knock doors, and work a little harder.

Jesus said, "I've ordained you from the foundation of the world to work." I'm not interested in how you feel; I'm interested in how you work. Work until Jesus comes. Jesus says, "I don't care what kinds of feelings you have, I want works done. I ordained you to work."

When you stand in Heaven, the Bible says you'll be judged for what works you did, not what feelings you had. "Well, I didn't know how people would receive it. I didn't want to offend anybody." God says, "I don't care what people feel like. I care about the works I asked you to do."

Jesus said in John 9:4, *"I must work the works of him that sent me, while it is day: the night cometh, when no man can work."* Work that bus route. Work that Sunday school class. Work your adult Sunday school class. Work that nursing home ministry. Work that Bible Club. Work that truck stop ministry. Work that Sailor Ministry. Do the works!

Say, "God, I'm asking a hard thing. I want a double portion. Yes, You heard me." What right do I have to do that? The life verse I adopted two years ago, Ephesians 3:20,

"Now unto him that is able to do exceeding abundantly above all that we ask or think,..." what are you asking? I'm asking for a double portion, and God says, "I can beat that." Are you able? God says, "The ability is not the issue."

I'm not worried about God's ability. I'm worried about God's willingness. It doesn't say, "Now unto him that is willing to do it," it says, "Now unto him that is able to do." The willingness is our bending His arm, twisting His ear, and saying, "God, I have caught the right spirit, and I'm willing to do the work. Will you please now use Your ability?" God says, "That's what I'm looking for. I'm looking for you to make Me want to do what I'm able to do."

3. Stay close to where God is doing the great works. Elijah and Elisha were shadowed by the sons of the prophets, a group of theologians and denominational leaders. Elijah was busy doing the works, traveling to all the different places, and Elisha was told to leave him and go on. Elisha said, "No, I'm going to stay right by you." Elijah said, "You better stay by me because if you see me when I go, you'll get your wish of a double portion." There was a group of people who were not close to him. It was a little handful of 50 preacher boys in a denominational college not doing much. They followed afar off and mocked Elisha. When Elijah went to Heaven, Elisha was next to him, and he caught that mantle. He did 12 miracles and prophesied four times. He received the double portion. Why? Because he was where God was doing the works.

A man came to Jesus, and Jesus said, "If any man be My disciple, follow Me." He said, "I want to follow You. I will follow You, but I've got to go home and bury my father and mother." Now, every Bible teacher knows his mom and dad hadn't died. He wasn't going home for a funeral service. He was going home to wait for them to die and take care of them in their old age. Jesus said, "Let the dead bury the

dead. You stay by Me. This is where the work is happening."
He said, "What about my family?" Jesus said, "You better
decide who your family is."

I'm going to make a bold statement here, "My family,"
Jesus said, "are those who do the will of My Father." God
wasn't minimizing your taking care of your mom and dad.
God said you're supposed to take care of them, but a whole
lot of you are going to lose the greatest place of blessing
since the book of Acts. You're going to go to some dried-up,
dead, boring, old church that hasn't had a baptistery
opened. They've got cobwebs and mice in their baptistery.
There's not been one baptism in that church in over six
months. There's nobody getting saved. There's no altar
filled with the tears of people getting right with God and
repenting. You're going to go there because a mom and dad
who are in their sixties, seventies, or eighties, and you're
going to say, "I've got to take care of mom and dad." You
move mom and dad where the blessings of God are.

There comes a point when you say to an aging mom and
dad, "I will take care of you, but guess who the parent is
now? I am."

I've told my parents, "When you can't take care of yourselves, I won't be moving to Holland, Michigan." Do you
think as the pastor of this church I'd say, "Folks, I've got to
resign and take care of my mommy and daddy." They'll be
moving down by me, because I'm not going to leave the
place where God has ordained His blessings and used me in
a profound way.

Some of you are going to walk out of the blessings of
God in the name of taking care of your mother or father.
Get them from where they are and put them in the retire-
ment village we're building now. Move them here, and let
them see what the power of God is all about. Let them see
the blessings of God. Let them see the windows of Heaven

open up Sunday morning, Sunday night, and Wednesday night. Let them see the altar packed with more people than they ever had in their church.

Where else are you going to have eight, nine, ten, eleven, twelve, or thirteen thousand people getting baptized? By the way, the day is going to come when it will be eighteen, nineteen, twenty, twenty-one, twenty-two, twenty-three, twenty-four, or twenty-five thousand baptisms. You're going to want to be here when it happens, and don't you say, "I've always loved the soil back home." I don't care about dirt. I want the blessings of God! Some of you are making the stupidest mistake of your life.

"Well, Mom and Dad are getting up there." You just want to get lazy and go fishing.

Hammond is where it is happening, and a whole lot of you folks have the blessings all mixed up. You think, "Well, after you put in 20 or 25 years at First Baptist Church of Hammond, you've done your time." What do you think this is, prison? What do you think this is, an institution? You've been sentenced to Hammond?

I remember what I felt like the first time I walked in this auditorium. I felt as though my whole hometown could fit in here. All my Dutch relatives could fit in here. You remember how you felt when you walked inside here. Wait until you walk in the new auditorium. You're going to say, "You've got to be kidding." God says, "I'm ready to sweat, how about you?"

Some of you can't wait. "Four more years, and I'm done with the steel mills, and then we can go back." Go back to what? Some dead Southern Baptist Church because it's the closest thing within 45 minutes? Some independent Baptist Church run by some guy who runs a full-time trucking business and preaches on the side because he can't do anything better? Or you'll stumble over somebody accidentally getting saved because they're begging to get saved?

I know what it's like to have a baptistery where you've got to clean the choir out, and get all the chairs off, and push the baptistery floor up, and fill it up that afternoon because somebody's going to get baptized. It only happens about every three or four months. We were a pretty hot thing in town. Bless God, something like this where every Sunday morning and Sunday night those waters are stirring—where are you gonna find this?

Bless God, you stay here. You go to God, and you say, "God, I'm going to stay where the blessings are. I'm going to stay where Your power is. I'm going to stay where Elijah has been. I'm going to stay where the blessings of God are falling down. I'm going to die here. I'm going to build that bus route here. I'm going to build my Sunday school class here. I'm not going to go home and watch grandma molt.

I think going home to take care of your parents is an excuse you're hiding behind, and you're going to miss out on the greatest days, and the greatest growth of First Baptist Church of Hammond. We're not going to do better works than what God used Brother Hyles to do. We're just going to do more of the same old stuff. I plan on staying around, how about you?